Colourful Crochet

Colourful Crochet

35 DESIGNS TO BRING THE BENEFITS OF COLOUR INTO YOUR LIFE

EMMA LEITH

CICO BOOKS

LONDON NEW YORK

Published in 2021 by CICO Books
an imprint of Ryland Peters & Small Ltd
20–21 Jockey's Fields,
London WC1R 4BW

www.rylandpeters.com

10 9 8 7 6 5 4 3 2 1

Text © Emma Leith 2021
Design, illustration, and photography ©
CICO Books 2021

A CIP catalogue record for this book is
available from the British Library.

ISBN: 978-1-78249-893-3

Printed in China

Editor: Marie Clayton
Pattern checker: Jemima Bicknell
Photographer: James Gardiner
Stylist: Nel Haynes
Illustrator: Stephen Dew

Art director: Sally Powell
Head of production: Patricia Harrington
Publishing manager: Penny Craig
Publisher: Cindy Richards

Contents

Introduction 6

Chapter 1 Spring **8**

Springtime Table Runner 10
Beach-hut Bunting 13
Coat Hangers 16
Floral Tiles Cushion 18
Gift Tags 22
Spring Blossom 24
Winter Turns to Spring
  Necklace 26

Chapter 2 Summer **28**

Carnival Shelf Valance 30
Colourplay Face Scrubbies 34
Summer Spice Tassel
  Key Rings 36
Zipped Make-up Bags 38
Summer Love Wall Hanging 40
Mandala Cushion 43

Chapter 3 Autumn **46**

Woodland Walk Shoulder
  Bag 48
Patchwork Gloves 51
Dingle Dangle Garland 54
Striped Purses 58
Season's End Scarf 60
Speckled Cowl 62
Twisted Headband 64

Chapter 4 Winter **66**

Neon Mandalas 68
Blue Tile Trivet 71
Bobble Cushion 74
Bobble Hat 76
Rope Baskets 78
Dreamcatcher 80
Snowdrift Throw 83

Chapter 5 Four Seasons **86**

Vase of Flowers 88
Moroccan Floor Cushion 91
Festival Bunting 94
Yarn-bombed Stool 97
Namaste Heart 100
Festive Baubles 104
Balloon Bauble Bunting 106
Granny Bag 108

Techniques 111
Suppliers 127
Acknowledgements 127
Index 128

Introduction

Confession time – I am no expert and I have no formal training. The one thing I am qualified in is feeling from the heart and knowing what I like. This has been the guiding force throughout my life and so far, it seems to be working! This book is a window into my colourful world – and it is my sincerest wish to infect you with a love of colour too, so that you can experience the mood-shifting qualities that colours can bring.

When faced with the cornucopia of colourful yarn available to us it is easy to feel a little daunted and overwhelmed and not know where to begin, so I have created these 35 projects for all abilities to allow you to explore colour with confidence. Taking inspiration from the seasonal colour changes that occur in nature, the projects are divided into the four seasons with their appropriate colour palettes. A fifth chapter incorporates all the colours under the title 'Four Seasons'. This last chapter was so that I could dive into the full palette and play to my heart's content… happily the good people at CICO Books said yes!

My natural go-to colour combo is hot pink and deep orange, as I love the vibrant energy they bring. Looking around my home it's easy to identify my leaning towards these warm summery shades… there are very few neutrals in our household! This is not to say I don't also enjoy immersing myself in the calming essence of the blue and aqua hues, but until recently I had always stuck to these two contrasting palettes. When I was commissioned to create a project working with the earthier autumnal tones, it was a joyful revelation to me. Who knew mustard and sage could be so delicious? (I now use mustard in just about everything!) What I experienced was the delight of stepping outside my comfort zone and seeing the world light up in a way it hadn't done until then. I encourage you to do the same and enjoy the pleasures of something new. Now is the time to embrace the rainbow.

May this book encourage and inspire you on your colourful crochet journey.

Namaste.

chapter 1

Spring

Springtime Table Runner

This table runner has it all when it comes to springtime colours, like a bouquet packed with daffodils and roses, peonies and hyacinths. The twisted baker's twine yarn that gets woven in at the end is where the magic really happens. Not only does it create a fabulous textured effect, but it also sets the colours off beautifully, sometimes popping and other times complementing, but always working in harmony no matter what.

Skill level: **

YARN AND MATERIALS

Scheepjes Cahlista Aran Cotton (100% natural cotton, 85m/93yd per 50g/1¾ oz ball) Aran (worsted) weight yarn:
2 balls of Bridal White shade 105 (A)

  1 ball each of:
  Crystalline shade 385 (B)
  Tulip shade 222 (C)
  Lemon shade 280 (D)
  Lavender shade 520 (E)
  Lemonade shade 403 (F)
  Shocking Pink shade 114 (G)
  Lilac Mist shade 399 (H)
  Jade shade 514 (I)
  Lime Juice shade 392 (J)
  Apple Granny shade 513 (K)

HOOKS AND EQUIPMENT

4mm (US size G/6) crochet hook

Yarn needle

FINISHED MEASUREMENTS

122cm (48in) long x 25cm (10in) wide

TENSION

12 htr x 10 rows measures 7 x 10cm (2¾ x 4in) working half treble using a 4mm (US size G/6) hook.

ABBREVIATIONS

See page 127.

SPECIAL ABBREVIATIONS

3trCL (3-treble cluster): [yarn round hook, insert hook in stitch, yarn round hook, pull through the work, yarn round hook, pull through two loops on hook] 3 times in same stitch, yarn round hook and draw through all 4 loops on hook to complete the cluster
edc (extended double crochet): work a double crochet stitch in the next dc two rows below

Table runner

Carry yarn not being worked at back of work, crocheting over it as you go.

Foundation chain: Using A, ch43.

BLOCK 1

Row 1: 1dc in second ch from hook, 1dc in each ch to end. (*42 dc*)

Note: On subsequent repeats of rows 1–23, work row 1 as: Ch1 (does not count as a st), 1dc in each st to end.

Row 2: Using block colour from list, ch3 (counts as first tr), 1tr in each st to end. (*42 tr*)

Row 3: Using A, ch1 (does not count as a st), 1dc in each st to end. (*42 dc*)

Row 4 (RS): Using A, ch2 (does not count as a st), *1htr in next st, change block colour from list, 3trCL in next st, change to A, 1htr in next st; rep from * to end, fasten off block colour leaving A for next row.

Row 5: Rep row 3.

Row 6: Rep row 2.

Row 7: Using A, ch2 (does not count as a st), 1htr in each st to end. (*42 htr*)

Row 8: Rep row 3.

Row 9: Using block colour from list, ch1 (does not count as a st), 1dc in each st to end. (*42 dc*)

Row 10: Using block colour from list, ch1 (does not count as a st), *1dc in next st, 1edc into next dc from 2 rows below; rep from * to end.

Row 11: Using block colour from list, ch3 (counts as first tr), 1tr in each st to end. (*42 tr*)

Row 12: Using A, ch1 (does not count as a st), 1dc in each st to end. (*42 dc*)

Row 13: Using A, ch2 (does not count as a st), 1htr in each st to end. (*42 htr*)

Row 14: Using block colour from list, ch3 (counts as first tr), 1tr in each st to end. (*42 tr*)

Row 15: Using block colour from list, ch1 (does not count as a st), 1dc in each st to end. (*42 dc*)

Row 16: Rep row 14.

Row 17: Using A, ch1 (does not count as a st), 1dc in each st to end. (*42 dc*)

Row 18: Using A, ch2 (does not count as a st), 1htr in each st to end. (*42 htr*)

Row 19: Using block colour from list, ch1 (does not count as a st), 1dc in each st to end. (*42 dc*)

Colour combinations

The runner is made up of six sections, each worked to the same pattern but in the different colour combinations detailed below. At the end of block 6, rows 1–5 of block 1 are repeated – this creates a symmetrically balanced table runner.

BLOCK 1

Rows 1, 3, 5, 7, 8, 12, 13, 17, 18 and 22	Yarn A
Rows 2 and 6	Yarn B
Row 4	Yarns A and C
Row 9	Yarn D
Rows 10 and 11	Yarn E
Rows 14 and 16	Yarn F
Row 15	Yarn D
Row 19	Yarn G
Rows 20 and 21	Yarn C

BLOCK 2

Rows 1, 3, 5, 7, 8, 12, 13, 17, 18 and 22	Yarn A
Rows 2 and 6	Yarn H
Row 4	Yarns A and G
Row 9	Yarn B
Rows 10 and 11	Yarn I
Rows 14 and 16	Yarn C
Row 15	Yarn E
Row 19	Yarn G
Rows 20 and 21	Yarn J

BLOCK 3

Rows 1, 3, 5, 7, 8, 12, 13, 17, 18 and 22	Yarn A
Rows 2 and 6	Yarn K
Row 4	Yarns A and D
Row 9	Yarn E
Rows 10 and 11	Yarn G
Rows 14 and 16	Yarn H
Row 15	Yarn E
Row 19	Yarn I
Rows 20 and 21	Yarn B

BLOCK 4

Rows 1, 3, 5, 7, 8, 12, 13, 17, 18 and 22	Yarn A
Rows 2 and 6	Yarn C
Row 4	Yarns A and K
Row 9	Yarn I
Rows 10 and 11	Yarn B
Rows 14 and 16	Yarn H
Row 15	Yarn E
Row 19	Yarn E
Rows 20 and 21	Yarn G

BLOCK 5

Rows 1, 3, 5, 7, 8, 12, 13, 17, 18 and 22	Yarn A
Rows 2 and 6	Yarn K
Row 4	Yarns A and D
Row 9	Yarn G
Rows 10 and 11	Yarn J
Rows 14 and 16	Yarn C
Row 15	Yarn E
Row 19	Yarn B
Rows 20 and 21	Yarn I

BLOCK 6

Rows 1, 3, 5, 7, 8, 12, 13, 17, 18 and 22	Yarn A
Rows 2 and 6	Yarn H
Row 4	Yarns A and G
Row 9	Yarn G
Rows 10 and 11	Yarn C
Rows 14 and 16	Yarn F
Row 15	Yarn D
Row 19	Yarn D
Rows 20 and 21	Yarn E

Tips

• Change to the new colour on the last yarn round hook of the current row unless otherwise stated. When joining and fastening off leave 15cm (6in) tail ends to sew into the back of your work to fasten securely.

• The contrast before and after weaving yarns is quite something, and I encourage you to play around with different colour combinations for the weaving threads to see just how the colours work with each other.

Row 20: Using block colour from list, ch1 (does not count as a st), *1dc in next st, 1edc into next htr in row 18; rep from * to end.

Row 21: Using block colour from list, ch3 (counts as first tr), 1tr in each st to end. (*42 tr*)

Row 22: Using A, ch2 (does not count as a st), 1htr in each st to end.

BLOCK 2
Rep rows 1 to 22 using block 2 colours.

BLOCK 3
Rep rows 1 to 22 using block 3 colours.

BLOCK 4
Rep rows 1 to 22 using block 4 colours.

BLOCK 5
Rep rows 1 to 22 using block 5 colours.

BLOCK 6
Rep rows 1 to 22 using block 6 colours.

Rep rows 1–5 of block 1, then rep row 3 once.
Fasten off.

Making up and finishing

Sew in all ends.

BORDER
Join A in first dc of final row. Ch1 (counts as first dc), *1dc in each st to corner, (ch2, 1dc) in same st (first corner made), 1dc in each dc and each htr post and 2dc in each tr post to the first dc of row 1, (1dc, ch2, 1dc) in this st (next corner made); rep from * once more, ending with 1dc in same st as first dc, ss in beg ch-1 to join.
Fasten off and sew in ends.

WEAVING AND
SURFACE CROCHET
Choose any contrasting colour and with RS facing, work surface crochet over half treble rows.
Using a yarn needle, thread two contrasting colours together and join into the back of your work to secure. Twist the threads together between thumb and finger to create a baker's twine effect and weave it through all the treble posts. Sew in the ends to secure.

Beach-hut Bunting

This miniature bunting is inspired by the rows of colourful beach huts that adorn our coastal regions, looking magnificent in their bright pastel shades. Each little bunting triangle combines soft tones of sea blues and summer pinks with minty greens and sandy yellows to create a string of mini bunting that can be hung just about anywhere.

Skill level: **

YARN AND MATERIALS

Scheepjes Catona 10g (100% cotton, approx. 25m/27yd per 10g/⅓oz ball) 4-ply (sport) weight yarn:
  1 ball each of:
  Tulip shade 222 (A)
  Powder Pink shade 238 (B)
  English Tea shade 404 (C)
  Bluebell shade 173 (D)
  Bluebird shade 247 (E)
  Cyan shade 397 (F)
  Crystalline shade 385 (G)
  Tropic shade 253 (H)
  Lemon Chiffon shade 100 (J)
  Lilac Mist shade 399 (K)
  Light Orchid shade 226 (L)
  Apricot shade 524 (M)
  Lemonade shade 403 (N)
  Yellow Gold shade 208 (P)

HOOKS AND EQUIPMENT

3mm (US size C/2–D/3) crochet hook

Stitch marker

Yarn needle

FINISHED MEASUREMENTS

Each triangle: 5cm (2in) at widest point x 7cm (2¾in) in length
Finished length of bunting: 90cm (36in)

TENSION

15 sts x 10 rows measures 7cm (2¾in) square working half treble using a 3mm (US size C/2–D/3) hook.

ABBREVIATIONS

See page 127.

COLOUR THERAPY

Some of the triangles have two colours, others have as many as seven, creating nautical stripes that are reminiscent of deck-chair fabric. The tones all complement each other, so as you make your bunting you can be confident of any colour combination that you choose. After finishing your triangles, notice how the little dots of contrasting colour made when adding the French knots can completely alter the look and feel of the original piece.

Colour combinations

TRIANGLE 1	Triangle	French knots
Rows 1–5	Yarn C	Yarn D
Rows 6–11	Yarn A	Yarn N
Ball	Yarn P	

TRIANGLE 2	Triangle	French knots
Rows 1–4	Yarn D	Yarns J and P
Rows 5–7	Yarn E	Yarn A
Rows 8–11	Yarn F	Yarn B
Ball	Yarn C	

TRIANGLE 3	Triangle
Row 1	Yarn J
Rows 2–3	Yarn G
Row 4	Yarn K
Rows 5–6	Yarn B
Row 7	Yarn L
Rows 8–9	Yarn P
Rows 10–11	Yarn J
Ball	Yarn G

TRIANGLE 4	Triangle	French knots
Rows 1–4	Yarn H	Yarns J and A
Rows 5–11	Yarn G	Yarn P
Ball	Yarn M	

TRIANGLE 5	Triangle
Rows 1–2	Yarn L
Row 3	Yarn J
Rows 4–5	Yarn M
Row 6	Yarn G
Rows 7–8	Yarn A
Rows 9–11	Yarn B
Ball	Yarn E

TRIANGLE 6	Triangle	French knots
Rows 1–2	Yarn G	Yarns P and N throughout
Rows 3–5	Yarn L	
Rows 6–11	Yarn B	
Ball	Yarn H	

TRIANGLE 7	Triangle	French knots
Rows 1–3	Yarn E	Yarns C and D
Row 4	Yarn P	
Rows 5–8	Yarn K	
Rows 10–11	Yarn J	
Ball	Yarn A	

Triangle

(make 10, one in each colour combination)
This is the pattern for the triangle to be used throughout, following colour change combinations as written above.
Foundation chain: Using row 1 colour, ch12.
Row 1: 1htr in third ch from hook, 1htr in each of next 9 sts. (*10 htr*)
Row 2: Ch2 (does not count as st throughout), miss next st, 1htr in each st to end. (*9 htr*)
Row 3: As row 2. (*8 htr*)
Row 4: As row 2. (*7 htr*)
Row 5: As row 2. (*6 htr*)
Row 6: As row 2. (*5 htr*)
Row 7: As row 2. (*4 htr*)
Row 8: As row 2. (*3 htr*)
Row 9: As row 2. (*2 htr*)
Row 10: Ch2, miss next st, 1htr in last st. (*1 htr*)
Row 11: Ch1, ss in next st.
Fasten off.

Ball

(make one for each triangle in yarn A, C, N, L, D, H, G, E, M, P)
Leaving a 15cm (6in) tail for stuffing the ball, make a magic ring.

Round 1: 6dc into ring. (*6 dc*)
Work in a continuous spiral, PM in last st and move up as each round is finished.
Round 2: 2dc in each st to end. (*12 dc*)
Round 3: 1dc in each st to end.
Round 4: *dc2tog; rep from * to end. (*6 dc*)
Stuff ball with tail end.
Round 5: 1dc in next st, [dc2tog] 3 times removing marker, ss in next st. (*3 sts*)
Fasten off and use long end to close hole.

Making up and finishing

Embellish each triangle with French knots (see page 123) in the yarn colours as given in colour combinations.
HANGING CORD
Using D, ch15, ss in 15th ch from hook to make a large loop, ch10, pick up first triangle, *with RS facing, 1dc in each st across top edge of triangle, ch6, pick up next triangle; rep from * until all triangles have been joined, ch25, ss in 15th ch from hook to form a large loop.
Fasten off.
Sew in ends.

TRIANGLE 8	Triangle	French knots
Rows 1–4	Yarn C	Yarns D and E
Rows 5–7	Yarn M	
Rows 8–11	Yarn K	
Ball	Yarn N	

TRIANGLE 9	Triangle	French knots
Rows 1~3	Yarn A	Yarn G
Rows 4~8	Yarn N	Yarn A
Rows 911	Yarn G	Yarn N
Ball	Yarn L	

Triangle 10	Triangle
Row 1	Yarn M
Rows 2–3	Yarn K
Row 4	Yarn A
Rows 5–6	Yarn J
Row 7	Yarn G
Rows 8–9	Yarn B
Rows 10–11	Yarn H
Ball	Yarn D

Tip
• Change colour on last yarn round hook of last half-treble in current row.

Coat Hangers

These four hangers, inspired by spring greens and blossom pinks, demonstrate how colours can be altered depending upon the colours they sit against. As well as the effect of the single stripe colours, the green and white French knots lift the lacy edging of the green hanger, while the pinks against the deep aqua blues of the other hanger deepen the overall effect.

Skill level: **

YARN AND MATERIALS

Scheepjes Catona (100% cotton, approx. 63m/68yd per 25g/⅞oz ball) 4-ply (sport) weight yarn:

1 ball each of:
Bridal White shade 105 (A)
Powder Pink shade 238 (B)
Tulip shade 222 (C)
Fresia shade 519 (D)
Light Orchid shade 226 (E)
Shocking Pink shade 114 (F)
Bluebell shade 173 (G)
Bluebird shade 247 (H)
Crystalline shade 385 (I)
Tropic shade 253 (J)
Apple Granny shade 513 (K)
Lime Juice shade 392 (L)
Cyan shade 397 (M)

HOOKS AND EQUIPMENT

3mm (US size C/2–D/3) crochet hook

Yarn needle

FINISHED MEASUREMENTS

To fit 31cm (12½in) wooden coat hanger
Actual size: 30cm (12in) long x 7cm (2¾in) wide before being fitted to hanger

TENSION

13 dc x 7 rows measures 7 x 3cm (2¾ x 1¼in) working double crochet using a 3mm (US size C/2–D/3) hook.

Hanger

Foundation chain: Ch14.
Row 1: 1dc in second ch from hook, 1dc in each ch to end. (*13 dc*)
Row 2: Ch1 (does not count as a st), 1dc in each st to end.
Work to required length of coat hanger ensuring work is slightly shorter than hanger.
Fasten off.

COLOUR THERAPY

This is a lovely little project for you to experiment with and experience the interplay of colours. Each hanger is comprised of stripes and the dividing stripe is always only one row of double crochet. It's the colour of this stripe that we are interested in: notice how the pink dividing stripes that separate the blue and green stripes (made up of 2, 3 or 4 rows of double crochet) in hanger number 2 completely alter the overall effect when compared to the white dividing stripe. The white dividing stripes between the colours in hangers number 1 and 2 give an overall freshness to them, lifting them and giving them space to breathe.

Making up and finishing

Fold the strip in half lengthways with RS together and sew the short ends together. Turn inside out. Lay flat and place the hanger onto the work to find the position of the hanger hook. Push the hanger hook through the centre of the cover from inside to fit it onto the hanger. Sew along the bottom edge using any colour yarn to secure the hanger inside.

EDGING
Work in multiples of 4 plus 1.
Row 1: Join the edging yarn at one end of the sewn seam and work 61 dc along the seam to the other end.
Row 2: Ss in first st, *miss next st, 4htr in next st, miss next st, ss in next st; rep from * to end.
Fasten off.
Make French knots (see page 123) in the centre of each htr grouping.

Colour combinations

HANGER 1
Alternating any pink with any blue or green separated by one row of yarn A, following the sequencing as for hanger 2
Edging in yarn H with French knots in A and F

HANGER 2
All of the greens with a one-row stripe of yarn A between each shade of green stripe. Each green stripe can be either 2, 3 or 4 rows
Edging in yarn K with French knots worked alternately in yarns L and A

HANGER 3
Pink stripes with one row stripes of yarns G, I, J or M, following the sequencing as above
Edging in yarn A with French knots worked in yarns I and J

HANGER 4
Blues and greens with one row of pink (yarns B, C or D) between each blue or green stripe. Each blue or green stripe can be either 2, 3 or 4 rows
Edging in yarn M with French knots worked in yarns C and E

Floral Tiles Cushion

Here's a different way of working with a print yarn that maximises a range of colours from just one ball – don't just use the yarn as it comes, but feel free to pull it on to reach the colours you want. I preferred to keep the colours as bright as possible – I didn't use too much of the dark jade, preferring the brighter yellow and orange.

Skill level: ***

YARN AND MATERIALS

West Yorkshire Spinners ColourLab DK (100% pure British wool, approx. 225m/245yd per 100g/3½oz ball) DK (light worsted) weight yarn:
  1 ball each of:
  Prism Brights shade 894 (A)
  Summer Pinks shade 893 (B)
  2 balls of Arctic White shade 011 (C)

45 x 45cm (18 x 18in) cushion with white cotton zipped cover

HOOKS AND EQUIPMENT

4mm (US size G/6) crochet hook

Yarn needle

Sewing needle and white thread to sew crochet to cushion

FINISHED MEASUREMENTS

45 x 45cm (18 x 18in)

TENSION

Rounds 1–3 of Foundation Square measure 6cm (2⅜in) square using a 4mm (US size G/6) hook.

ABBREVIATIONS

See page 127.

SPECIAL ABBREVIATIONS

3dtrCL (3-double treble cluster): *yarn round hook twice, insert hook in stitch, yarn round hook, pull through the work, [yarn round hook, pull through 2 loops on the hook] twice; rep from * twice more, yarn round hook, pull through all loops on hook to complete cluster

etr (extended treble): work a treble stitch in the next dc two rows below

FPtrtr (front post triple treble): working from the front, yarn round hook 3 times, insert hook from front to back to front around post of stitch in row below, yarn round hook, draw yarn around post of stitch (5 loops on hook), [yarn round hook, pull through 2 loops on hook] 4 times

Tips

• It is possible to make two flower centres (rounds 1 and 2) from each colour strip before the yarn changes to the next colour.

• Don't tighten the magic ring fully until round 2 of the square has been worked – this will allow space for the extended treble.

Foundation square

Using any colour from A or B, make a magic ring.

Round 1: Ch4 (counts as first dtr in 3dtrCL), *yrh twice, insert hook into ring, yrh, pull through work, [yrh, pull through 2 loops on hook] twice; rep from * once more, yrh, pull through all loops on hook (first 3dtrCL complete), ch8, [3dtrCL into ring, ch8] 3 times, ss in top of beg ch-4 to join. (*Four 3dtrCL + 4 ch-8 sps*)

Fasten off.

In next round you will be working over the ch-8 as you make etr in the central ring.

Round 2: Join C at top of any 3dtrCL, ch2 (counts as first dc and ch-1 sp), (1etr, ch2, 1etr) in ring, ch1, [1dc in top of next 3dtrCL, ch1, (1etr, ch2, 1etr) in ring, ch1] 3 times, ss in top of beg ch-2 to join. (*12 sts + 4 ch-2 sps + 8 ch-1 sps*)

Round 3: Ss in first ch-1 sp, ch1 (counts as first dc), *(3htr, ch2, 3htr) in next ch-2 sp, (first corner made), 1dc in next ch-1 sp, ch1, miss next dc, 1dc in next ch-1 sp; rep from * twice more, (3htr, ch2, 3htr) in next ch-2 sp (last corner made), 1dc in next ch-1 sp, ch1, miss next dc, ss in beg ch-1 to join.

Fasten off.

Current square

Using any colour from A or B, make a magic ring.
Rep rounds 1 and 2 of foundation square.

JOIN SQUARES
Beg working join-as-you-go (see page 122) on round 3 to join squares tog.

Round 3: Ss in first ch-1 sp, ch1 (counts as first dc), (3htr, ch2, 3htr) in next ch-2 sp (first corner made), 1dc in next ch-1 sp, ch1, miss next dc, 1dc in next ch-1 sp, 3htr in next ch-2 sp, insert hook in corner sp of foundation square from underneath, 1dc in corner sp of foundation square (counts as first of ch-2 for corner sp), ch1, work second 3-htr grouping in corner sp of current square, 1dc in next ch-1 sp of current square, 1dc in ch-1 sp of foundation square (counts as ch-1 for current square), miss next dc of current square, 1dc in next ch-1 sp of current square, 3htr in next ch-2 sp of current square, 1dc in corner sp of foundation square (counts as first of ch-2 for corner sp), ch1, work second 3-htr grouping in corner sp of current square, cont to work around current square as set for round 3.

Make another 34 current squares to make 6 rows of 6 squares for central piece. When joining to two previous squares, replace both corner ch of current square with 1dc in each adjoining square.

BORDER
Round 1: Join C in any ch-2 corner sp of piece, ch3 (counts as first tr throughout), 2tr in same sp (half corner made), ch1, [miss next 3 htr, 3tr in next dc, ch1, miss next ch-1 sp and 1 dc, 3tr in sp between dc and 3-htr group, ch1, miss 3 htr, 3tr in sp between joined squares, ch1] 5 times, miss next 3 htr, 3tr in next dc, ch1, miss next ch-1 sp and 1 dc, 3tr in sp between dc and 3-htr group,

ch1, *(3tr, ch2, 3tr) in next ch-2 sp for corner, ch1, [miss next 3 htr, 3tr in next dc, ch1, miss next ch-1 sp and 1 dc, 3tr in sp between dc and 3-htr group, ch1, miss next 3 htr, 3tr in sp between joined squares, ch1] 5 times, miss next 3 htr, 3tr in next dc, ch1, miss next ch-1 sp and 1 dc, 3tr in sp between dc and 3-htr group, ch1; rep from * twice more, 3tr in same corner sp as beg half corner, ch2, ss in top of beg ch-3 to join.
Fasten off C.

Round 2: Join B in any ch-2 corner sp, ch3, 2tr in same sp (half corner made), *ch1, [3tr in next ch-1 sp, ch1] to next corner ch-2 sp, (3tr, ch2, 3tr) in ch-2 sp (corner made); rep from * twice more, ch1, [3tr in next ch-1 sp, ch1] to beg half corner, 3tr in same sp as beg half corner, ch2, ss in top of beg ch-3 to join.
Fasten off B.

Round 3: Join C in any ch-2 corner sp, ch3, 2tr in same ch-2 sp (half corner made), [(1tr, 1FPtrtr around post of middle tr from round 1, 1tr) in next ch-1 sp] to next ch-2 corner sp, (3tr, ch2, 3tr) in ch-2 sp (corner made); rep from * twice more, [(1tr, 1FPtrtr around post of middle tr from round 1, 1tr) in next ch-1 sp] to beg half corner, 3tr in same sp as beg half corner, ch2, join with a ss in top of beg ch-3.
Fasten off C.

Round 4: As round 2, using yarn B.

Round 5: Join yarn C in any ch-2 corner sp, ch1 (counts as first dc), 2dc in same ch-2 sp, 1dc in each of next 3 sts, *1FPtrtr around post of middle tr from round 3, 1dc in each of next 3 sts] to next ch-2 corner sp, 3dc in ch-2 corner sp, 1dc in each of next 3 sts; rep from * twice more, [1FPtrtr around post of middle tr from round 3, 1dc in each of next 3 sts] to end, ss in beg ch-1 to join.
Fasten off C.

Round 6: Join A in any st, work crab st as foll: ch1 (does not count as a st), working backward from left to right (for right-handed crochet, reverse if working left-handed), 1dc in each st to end, ss in beg dc to join.
Fasten off.

Making up and finishing

Sew in ends.
Sew crochet piece to one side of cotton cushion cover along top of round 3.

Gift Tags

Make the gift tag part of the gift with this little project that creates a decorative lace edging on any tag. My personal favourite here is the Lilac Mist tag – the pink and yellow French knots are bright and zingy, making them pop out beautifully.

Skill level: *

YARN AND MATERIALS

Scheepjes Maxi Sweet Treat (100% mercerised cotton, approx. 140m/153yd per 25g/⅞oz ball) 2-ply (lace) weight yarn:

  1 ball each of:
  Lemon shade 280 (A)
  Yellow Gold shade 208 (B)
  Spring Green shade 513 (C)
  Jade shade 514 (D)
  Fuchsia shade 786 (E)
  Tulip shade 222 (F)
  Light Orchid shade 226 (G)
  Crystalline shade 385 (H)
  Bridal White shade 105 (I)
  Icy Pink shade 246 (J)
  Lilac Mist shade 399 (K)

Brown kraft paper gift tags

HOOKS AND EQUIPMENT

1.5mm (US size 8 steel) crochet hook

Yarn needle

Sharp needle to make holes in tags

FINISHED MEASUREMENTS

Project is easily adjusted to fit chosen gift tag. Tags shown measure approx. 11cm (4¼in) long, 6cm (2¼in) wide

TENSION

Tension is not important for this project but stitches should be kept tight and dense.

ABBREVIATIONS

See page 127.

Tips

• You could create a decorative edge on a face cloth or other fabric pieces using the same pattern.

• The size of the crochet hook means it can be pushed through most lightweight fabrics.

Colour combinations

Tag 1	Yarns B and A
Tag 2	Yarns D and C
Tag 3	Yarns E and F
Tag 4	Yarn A with C and G French knots
Tag 5	Yarn H with I and J French knots
Tag 6	Yarn K with E and A French knots

Tags 1, 2 and 3

Measure and mark position of holes so they are evenly spaced about 0.5cm (¼in) apart around edge of each tag. Push a sharp yarn needle through each marked place to make holes.

Round 1: Join first colour in any hole, ch1 (does not count as st), 1dc in same hole, ch1, [1dc in next hole, ch1] around tag, working (1dc, ch2, 1dc) in each corner hole, ss in first dc to join.
Fasten off.

Round 2: Join second colour in any ch-1 sp, *ch3, 1htr in third ch from hook, miss next dc, ss in next sp; rep from * to end, ss in first ch of beg ch-3 to join.
Fasten off.

Tags 4, 5 and 6

Measure and mark position of holes so they are evenly spaced about 1cm (⅜in) apart around edge of each tag. Push a sharp yarn needle through each marked place to make holes.

Round 1: Join yarn in any hole, ch2 (counts as first htr), 2htr in same hole, ch1, [3htr in next hole, ch1] around tag, working (3htr, ch3, 3htr) in each corner hole, ss in top of beg ch-2 to join.
Fasten off.

DECORATION
Make first French knot (see page 123) in first hole to one side of main string hole at tip of tag, miss next hole. Repeat to make a French knot in every other hole around tag.
Fasten off. Repeat the process with second colour in rem holes.

Making up and finishing

Secure all ends neatly behind your work on the reverse side of the tags.

COLOUR THERAPY

Inspired by spring bouquets with a hint of warmth in their tone, the airy colours used sit in contrast to the classic brown tag, allowing the stitches to zing off the surface and give a happy feeling to the tags.

Spring Blossom

Bring a feeling of spring into your house at any time of the year with these pretty blooms arranged all over a simple bare branch. Arrange your mini balls of wool into a colour wheel and pick any colour as your flower centre. Now simply select the colour that is directly opposite – the complementary colour – for the petals in round 2.

Skill level: *

YARN AND MATERIALS

Scheepjes Catona 10g (100% cotton, approx. 25m/27yd per 10g/⅓oz ball) 4-ply (sport) weight yarn:

1 ball each of:
Cornelia Rose shade 256 (A)
Tulip shade 222 (B)
Powder Pink shade 238 (C)
Crystalline shade 385 (D)
Apple Granny shade 513 (E)
Lemon Chiffon shade 100 (F)
Lemon shade 280 (G)
Light Orchid shade 226 (H)

Small branch, painted white

Branch or twigs, painted or left natural

HOOKS AND EQUIPMENT

3mm (US size C/2–D/3) crochet hook

Yarn needle

Hot glue gun and glue sticks

FINISHED MEASUREMENTS

Each flower: 3cm (1¼in) diameter

TENSION

Rounds 1 and 2 measure 3cm (1¼in) diameter using a 3mm (US size C/2–D/3) hook.

ABBREVIATIONS

See page 127.

Tip

• Keep your tension tight and work over your tail ends as you go – give the tail a little tug at the end to pull the petals in.

COLOUR THERAPY

Complementary colours are colours that sit directly opposite each other on the colour wheel; when placed next to one another they create the strongest contrast and make each other appear brighter. Using complementary colours always creates an aesthetically pleasing result – and these little flowers play with this theory.

Flower

(make as many as required)
Using any centre colour, make a magic ring.
Round 1: Ch1 (does not count as a st), 10dc into ring, ss in first dc to join. (*10 sts*)
Fasten off centre colour.
Round 2: Join petal colour with a ss in any st, ch2, 1dtr in same st as ss, (1dtr, ch2, ss) in next st, [(ss, ch2, 1dtr) in next st, (1dtr, ch2, ss) in next st] 4 times.
Fasten off.

Making up and finishing

Sew in all ends.

Use the glue gun to fix flowers to the tips of twigs on the branch to create a floral spring display.

Winter Turns to Spring Necklace

This pretty necklace is made with a series of different-sized circles and beads arranged in a repeating sequence. Although many colours have been used, harmony is introduced by working the final round of three of the large circles and three of the small circles in white – this subtle colour pattern helps bring the whole piece together in a gentle way.

Skill level: **

YARN AND MATERIALS

Scheepjes Maxi Sweet Treat (100% mercerised cotton, approx. 140m/153yd per 25g/⅞oz ball) 2-ply (lace) weight yarn:
    1 ball each of:
    Lilac Mist shade 399 (A)
    Bluebell shade 173 (B)
    Sky Blue shade 510 (C)
    Bluebird shade 247 (D)
    Cyan shade 397 (E)
    Crystalline shade 385 (F)
    Spring Green shade 513 (G)
    Lemon shade 280 (H)
    Icy Pink shade 246 (I)
    Tulip shade 222 (J)
    Light Orchid shade 226 (K)
    Bridal White shade 105 (L)
    Yellow Gold shade 208 (M)

HOOKS AND EQUIPMENT

1.5mm (US size 8 steel) crochet hook

Small yarn needle

FINISHED MEASUREMENTS

53cm (21in) long

TENSION

Small circle (rounds 1–3) measures 2cm (⅞in) diameter using a 1.5mm (US size 8 steel) hook.

ABBREVIATIONS

See page 127.

Small circles

(make 9, using L for round 3 on three circles)
Using any colour, make a magic ring.
Round 1: Ch1 (does not count as a st), 6dc into ring, ss in first dc to join. (*6 dc*)
Fasten off first colour.
Round 2: Join second colour in any st, ch1 (counts as first dc throughout), 1dc in same st, 2dc in each st to end, ss in beg ch-1 to join. (*12 dc*)
Fasten off second colour.
Round 3: Join third colour in any st, ch1, 1dc in same st, [1dc in next st, 2dc in next st] 5 times, 1dc in next st, ss in beg ch-1 to join. (*18 dc*)
Fasten off.

Large circles

(make 9, using L for round 4 on three circles)
Rep rounds 1–3 of small circle.
Round 4: Join fourth colour in second st of any 2-dc inc, ch1, 1dc in next st, [2dc in next st, 1dc in each of next 2 sts] 5 times, 2dc in next st, ss in beg ch-1 to join. (*24 dc*)
Fasten off.

Beads

(make 6)
Using any colour, make a magic ring, leaving 10cm (4in) tail.
Round 1: Ch1 (does not count as a st), 5dc into ring. (*5 dc*)
Work in a continuous spiral.
Round 2: [2dc in next st] 5 times. (*10 dc*)
Round 3: 1dc in each of next 10 sts. (*10 dc*)
Round 4: [Dc2tog] twice, stuff bead with yarn tail, [dc2tog] 3 times. (*5 dc*)
Fasten off, weave tail in and out of rem sts, pull tight to close.

Tip

• Work over tail ends of each colour from previous round and pull to tighten the round. This keeps the tension tight and helps make the little circles hold their shape.

Making up and finishing

Arrange the circles in the following sequence: 1 large, 1 small, 1 large with border in L, 1 bead, 1 small, 1 large, 1 small with white border, 1 bead; repeat this sequence three times in total.

ASSEMBLE NECKLACE

Join A in any st of first large circle, ch10, join with a ss to next small circle.
Fasten off.
Count 9 sts around small circle and join A in last of these sts, ch10, ss to next large circle with border.
Fasten off.
Count 12 sts around large circle and join yarn A in last of these sts, ch10, cut yarn leaving 20cm (8in) tail. Thread next bead onto yarn up to ch st, ch10 with tail, ss to next small circle. Fasten off.
Cont as set, foll sequence laid out, until all pieces are joined, ending with a ch10. Ss to first circle to complete.

Sew in any ends.

COLOUR THERAPY

Every year without fail, as winter turns to spring and new life emerges from the earth, a peaceful joy fills my heart. The pale daffodil yellow, dusty pink and eggshell blue used in this project give a cool soft feel that reflect the tranquillity of this time of year. It's the use of the cooler Lilac Mist that keeps this necklace on the cusp of the seasonal change with its gentle lilac tone. Imagine how different it would feel if the joining colour were the warmer yellow or brighter pink; you may of course prefer this, in which case follow your heart!

chapter 2

Summer

Carnival Shelf Valance

Rich mandalas in sumptuous midsummer shades make this shelf valance one of my favourite pieces. Each mandala section is made up of one large and one small mandala with a crochet bauble and measures 22cm (8¾in), so you can adjust how many sections you will need to make to fit your own shelf.

Skill level: ✳✳✳

YARN AND MATERIALS

Scheepjes Cahlista Aran Cotton (100% natural cotton, approx. 85m/93yd per 50g/1¾oz ball) aran (worsted) weight yarn:

  1 ball each of:
  Bridal White shade 105 (A)
  Shocking Pink shade 114 (B)
  Royal Orange shade 189 (C)
  Yellow Gold shade 208 (D)
  Hot Red shade 115 (E)
  Deep Amethyst shade 508 (F)
  Cyan shade 397 (G)
  Vivid Blue shade 146 (H)
  Jade shade 514 (I)
  Apple Granny shade 513 (J)
  Ultra Violet shade 282 (K)
  Lavender shade 520 (L)
  Saffron shade 249 (M)

Rico Ricorumi Lamé DK (62% polyester, 38% polyamide, approx. 50m/54yd per 10g/⅓oz ball) DK (light worsted) weight yarn:
  1 ball of Gold shade 002

Decorating clips to hang

Fibrefill toy stuffing

HOOKS AND EQUIPMENT

4mm (US size G/6) crochet hook

Stitch markers

Yarn needle

PVA medium

FINISHED MEASUREMENTS

23cm (9in) deep (including crochet bauble), 125cm (50in) wide

TENSION

Rounds 1 and 2 of small mandala measure 5cm (2in) diameter using a 4mm (US size G/6) hook.

ABBREVIATIONS

See page 127.

SPECIAL ABBREVIATIONS

edc (extended double crochet): work a double crochet stitch in the next dc two rows below

FPhtr (front post half treble): working from the front, yarn round hook, insert hook from front to back to front around post of stitch in row below, yarn round hook, draw yarn around post of stitch (3 loops on hook), yarn round hook, pull through all 3 loops on hook

FPtr inc (front post treble increase): *working from the front, yarn round hook, insert hook from front to back to front around post of stitch in row below, yarn round hook, draw yarn around post of stitch, [yarn round hook, pull through 2 loops] twice; rep from * once more around same post

Large mandala

(make 5)
Using first colour, make a magic ring.
Round 1: Ch3 (counts as first tr), 11tr into ring, ss in beg ch-3 to join. (*12 tr*)
Fasten off first colour.
Round 2: Join second colour in any st, ch3 (counts as first tr), 1tr in same st, 2tr in each st to end, ss in top of ch-3 to join. (*24 sts*)
Fasten off second colour.
Round 3: Join third colour in any st, ch1 (counts as first dc), 1dc in next st, *ch3, 1dc in each of next 2 sts; rep from * to end, ch3, ss in beg ch-1 to join. (*24 dc + 12 ch-3 sps*)
Fasten off third colour.
Round 4: Join fourth colour in any ch-3 sp, ch2 (counts as first htr), *(1htr, 1tr, ch2, 1tr, 1htr) in next ch-3 sp; rep from * to end working (1htr, 1tr, ch2, 1tr) in last ch-3 sp, ss in top of beg ch-2 to join. (*48 sts + 12 ch-2 sps*)
Fasten off fourth colour.
Round 5: Join fifth colour in any ch-2 sp, ch6 (counts as first dc and ch-5 sp), *1dc in next ch-2 sp, ch5; rep from * to end, ss in first ch of beg ch-6 to join. (*12 dc + 12 ch-5 sps*)
Fasten off fifth colour.

LARGE MANDALA 1
Round 1	Yarn L
Round 2	Yarn D
Round 3	Yarn F
Round 4	Yarn B
Round 5	Yarn I
Round 6	Yarn C
Round 7	Yarn M with K as contrast

LARGE MANDALA 2
Round 1	Yarn G
Round 2	Yarn H
Round 3	Yarn B
Round 4	Yarn L
Round 5	Yarn K
Round 6	Yarn I
Round 7	Yarn C with M as contrast

LARGE MANDALA 3
Round 1	Yarn K
Round 2	Yarn B
Round 3	Yarn C
Round 4	Yarn F
Round 5	Yarn G
Round 6	Yarn H
Round 7	Yarn E with D as contrast

LARGE MANDALA 4
Round 1	Yarn B
Round 2	Yarn G
Round 3	Yarn K
Round 4	Yarn C
Round 5	Yarn D
Round 6	Yarn L
Round 7	Yarn I with J as contrast

LARGE MANDALA 5
Round 1	Yarn I
Round 2	Yarn F
Round 3	Yarn E
Round 4	Yarn K
Round 5	Yarn C
Round 6	Yarn M
Round 7	Yarn B with L as contrast

MINI MANDALA 1
Round 1	Yarn F
Round 2	Yarn I

MINI MANDALA 2
Round 1	Yarn K
Round 2	Yarn E

MINI MANDALA 3
Round 1	Yarn H
Round 2	Yarn J

MINI MANDALA 4
Round 1	Yarn G
Round 2	Yarn B

MINI MANDALA 5
Round 1	Yarn L
Round 2	Yarn D

MINI MANDALA 6
Round 1	Yarn M
Round 2	Yarn C

Round 6: Join sixth colour in any ch-5 sp, ch1 (counts as first dc), 4dc in same ch-5 sp, 1FPhtr around next dc, *5dc in next ch-5 sp, 1FPhtr around next dc; rep from * to end, ss in beg ch-1 to join. (*72 sts*)
Fasten off sixth colour.

Round 7: Join seventh colour in any dc after an FPhtr, ch2 (counts as first htr), 1htr in each of next 4 dc, join in contrast colour, FPtr inc in FPhtr from round 6, *change to seventh colour, 1htr in each of next 5 dc (first st may be 'hidden' behind FPtr inc so you may need to push it aside to find the st), change to contrast colour, FPtr inc in FPhtr from round 6; rep from * to end, ss in top of beg ch-2 to join. (*84 sts*)
Fasten off seventh and contrast colours.

Round 8: Join A in any st, ch4 (counts as first dc and ch-3 sp), miss next st, *1dc in next st, ch3, miss next st; rep from * to end, ss in first ch of beg ch-4 to join. (*42 dc + 42 ch-3 sps*)
Fasten off.

Mini mandalas
(make 6)
Using first colour, make a magic ring.
Round 1: Ch3 (counts as first tr throughout), 11tr into ring, ss in top of ch-3 to join. (*12 tr*)
Fasten off first colour.
Round 2: Join second colour in any st, ch3, 1tr in same st, 2tr in each st to end, ss in top of ch-3 to join. (*24 sts*)
Fasten off.

Large baubles
(make 1 each in J, B, C, D and L)
Make a magic ring.
Round 1: Ch1 (does not count as a st), 6dc into ring. (*6 dc*)
Work in a continuous spiral. PM in last st and move up as each round is finished.
Round 2: 2dc in each st to end. (*12 dc*)
Round 3: [1dc in next st, 2dc in next st] 6 times. (*18 sts*)
Round 4: 1dc in each st to end.
Round 5: [1dc in next st, dc2tog] 6 times. (*12 sts*)

Round 4: [Dc2tog] 6 times (fill with stuffing after third dc2tog).
Fasten off, weave tail in and out of rem sts, pull tight to close.

Mini baubles
(make 1 each in C, F, B, K, I and G)
Make a magic ring.
Round 1: Ch1 (does not count as a st), 6dc into ring. (*6 dc*)
Work in a continuous spiral. PM in last st and move up as each round is finished.
Round 2: 2dc in each st to end. (*12 dc*)
Round 3: 1dc in each st to end.
Round 4: [Dc2tog] 6 times.
Fasten off, weave tail in and out of rem sts, pull tight to close.

Making up and finishing
Sew in all ends.

DECORATE MANDALAS
Twist two contrasting strands of yarn together and weave into round 2 of each large and mini mandala.

Using Gold, work surface crochet around top of round 1 of each large and mini mandala.

JOIN MANDALAS

Lay all mandalas out with RS facing, in a line beginning and ending with a mini mandala. Start with the first mini mandala on the right:

Joining round: Join K in any st, ch4 (counts as first dc and ch-3 sp), miss next st, [1dc in next st, ch3, miss next st] twice, *1dc in next st, ch1, take next large mandala and work 1dc in any ch-3 sp to join two mandalas together, ch1, miss next st on mini mandala, cont to work [1dc in next st, ch3, miss next st] in mini mandala to end, ss in first ch of beg ch-4 to join. Fasten off K. Pick up next mini mandala and join C in any st, ch4 (counts as first dc and ch-3 sp), miss next st, [1dc in next st, ch3, miss next st] twice, 1dc in next st, ch1, take previously joined large mandala and count 12 ch-3 sps anti-clockwise from previous join, work 1dc in 13th ch-3 sp to join two mandalas together, ch1, miss next st on mini mandala, cont to work [1dc in next st, ch3, miss next st] into mini mandala 4 times.

Using yarns I, E, L, D in sequence, rep from * until all mandalas are joined.

Sew a large bauble to the bottom of each large mandala and a mini bauble to the bottom of each mini mandala.

TOP RUNNER

Take joined mandalas with RS facing and work from right to left, beg with first mini mandala as foll:

Row 1: Using B, ch4, 1tr in fourth ch-3 sp clockwise from where mini mandala joins large mandala, ch1, *[1htr in next ch-3 sp of mini mandala, ch1] twice, 1tr in next ch-3 sp of mini mandala, ch4, 1dtr in second ch-3 sp of large mandala anti-clockwise from where large mandala joins mini mandala, ch1, 1tr in next ch-3 sp, ch1, 1htr in next ch-3 sp, [ch1, 1dc in next ch-3 sp] 4 times, ch1, 1htr in next ch-3 sp, ch1, 1tr in next ch-3 sp, ch1, 1dtr in next ch-3 sp, miss last ch-3 sp before join, ch4, 1tr in next ch-3 sp of next mini mandala, ch1; rep from * 4 times, [1htr in next ch-3 sp of last mini mandala, ch1] twice, 1tr in next ch-3 sp of mini mandala, ch4, turn.

Row 2: 1dc in 2nd ch from hook, 1dc in each of next 2 ch, 1dc in each st and 1-ch sp, and 4dc in each ch-4 sp, to last 4 ch, 1dc in each of last 4 ch, fasten off B and join in L on last yrh, turn. (*184 dc*)

Row 3: Using L, ch2 (counts as first htr throughout), 1htr in same st, [miss 2 dc, 3htr in next st] 60 times, miss 2 dc, 2htr in last st, fasten off L and join in M on last yrh, turn.

COLOUR THERAPY

The combination of red, pink and orange with deep purples and blues gives a real heat to this project. The white border for the large mandala lifts the colours – were the white to be replaced with deep ultra violet instead, the overall effect would be to expand that summer heat, adding body and weight.

Row 4: Using M, ch2, [3htr in next sp between htr groups] 61 times, 2htr in 2nd of ch-2, fasten off M and join in C on last yrh, turn.

Row 5: Using C, ch2, 1htr in same st, miss first 3-tr group, [3htr in next sp between htr groups] 60 times, 2htr in 2nd of ch-2, fasten off C and join in K on last yrh.

Row 6: Using K, rep row 4, fasten off K and join in I on last yrh.

Row 7: Using I, rep row 5, fasten off I and join in A on last yrh.

Row 8: Using A, ch1 (does not count as a st), 1dc in each st to end, fasten off A and join in Gold on last yrh.

Row 9: Using Gold, ch1 (does not count as a st), 1dc in first st, 1edc in next st in row 7, *1dc in next st, 1edc in next st in row 7; rep from * to end.
Fasten off.

DECORATION

Using Gold, work surface crochet through row 2.
Using B, work surface crochet along top of row 7.
Fasten off and sew in any ends.

Colourplay Face Scrubbies

These little face scrubbies are the perfect way to practise using the colour wheel, showing how easy it is to select colours that harmonise. Pick any four colours that sit side by side on the wheel to make each scrubbie – it does not matter what order you work them in, so long as they all group together on the wheel. You will find the result looks very natural.

Skill level: **

YARN AND MATERIALS

Scheepjes Cahlista Aran Cotton (100% natural cotton, approx. 85m/93yd per 50g/1¾oz ball) aran (worsted) weight yarn:
1 ball each of:
Royal Orange shade 189 (A)
Yellow Gold shade 208 (B)
Lemon shade 280 (C)
Lemon Chiffon shade 100 (D)
Apple Granny shade 513 (E)
Jade shade 514 (F)
Crystalline shade 385 (G)

Cyan shade 397 (H)
Cornflower shade 511 (I)
Delphinium shade 113 (J)
Lavender shade 520 (K)
Tulip shade 222 (L)
Shocking Pink shade 114 (M)

HOOKS AND EQUIPMENT

4.5mm (US size 7) crochet hook

Yarn needle

FINISHED MEASUREMENTS

7.5cm (3in) diameter

TENSION

Round 1 measures 3cm (1¼in) diameter using a 4.5mm (US size 7) hook.

ABBREVIATIONS

See page 127.

SPECIAL ABBREVIATION

puff st (puff stitch): *yarn round hook, insert hook in stitch, yarn round hook and pull up a long loop; rep from * twice more in same stitch (7 loops on hook), yarn round hook and pull through all 7 loops on hook

Scrubby

Using first colour, make a magic ring.

Round 1: Ch1 (does not count as a st), [puff st into ring, ch1] 6 times, ss in top of first puff st to join. (6 puff sts)
Fasten off first colour.

Round 2: Join second colour in any ch-1 sp, ch1 (counts as first dc), 1dc in same sp, [1dc in top of next puff st, 2dc in next ch-1 sp] 5 times, 1dc in top of last puff st, ss in beg ch-1 to join. (18 sts)
Fasten off second colour.

Round 3: Join third colour in any dc, *puff st in next dc, ch1; rep from * to end, ss in top of first puff st to join.
Fasten off third colour.

Round 4: Join fourth colour in any ch-1 sp, ch1 (counts as first dc), 1dc in same sp, miss next puff st, *2dc in next ch-1 sp, miss next puff st; rep from * to end, ss in beg ch-1 to join. (36 sts)
Fasten off.

Making up and finishing

Sew in any ends.

Summer Spice Tassel Key Rings

Think Moroccan souks and Indian bazaar spice displays and you are tuned into the inspiration behind these mirrored tassel key rings. The colours combine to create a delicious feast for the eyes, vibrating with happiness and heat.

Skill level: **

YARN AND MATERIALS

Scheepjes Maxi Sweet Treat (100% mercerised cotton, approx. 140m/153yd per 25g/⅞oz ball) 2-ply (lace) weight yarn:

1 ball each of:
Spring Green shade 513 (A)
Fuchsia shade 786 (B)
Tangerine shade 281 (C)
Yellow Gold shade 208 (D)
Cyan shade 397 (E)
Ultra Violet shade 282 (F)
Jade shade 514 (G)

5cm (2in) diameter mirror for each tassel

Assorted glass seed beads (27 beads per mirrored tassel)

Clip key ring fixing for each tassel

HOOKS AND EQUIPMENT

1.5mm (US size 6 steel) crochet hook

Beading needle to thread beads onto cotton

Stitch marker

Yarn needle

FINISHED MEASUREMENTS

7cm (2¾in) diameter, 14cm (5½in) long (including tassel, excluding key ring fixing)

TENSION

Tension is not important for this project, but make sure the initial chain loop sits within circumference of mirror allowing for a 5mm (¼in) overlap.

ABBREVIATIONS

See page 127.

> ## Tip
> • Make sure your beads have a big enough hole so they can be threaded onto the yarn.

Mandala

(make 2 for each key ring)
Change yarn colour on each round in any sequence of your choosing.
Using first colour, ch30, ss in first ch to make large loop.
Round 1: Ch1 (does not count as a st throughout), working over yarn end as you go work 48dc in loop, ss in first dc to join. (*48 dc*)
Fasten off first colour. Gently pull yarn end to close loop slightly to make it tighter and evenly space dc before cont to next round.
Round 2: Join second colour in any st, ch1, 1dc in same st, ch2, miss next st, *1dc in next st, ch2, miss next st; rep from * to end, ss in first dc to join. (*24 dc + 24 ch-2 sps*)
Fasten off second colour.
Round 3: Join third colour in any missed st from round 2, ch1, 1dc in same st (working over ch-2 sp), ch2, miss next dc, *1dc in next missed st from round 2, ch2, miss next dc; rep from * to end, ss in top of first dc to join.
Fasten off third colour.
Rep to make second mandala.

JOIN MANDALAS

Hold two mandalas with WS tog, aligning ch-2 sps and working into both throughout.
Round 4: Join fourth colour in any ch-2 sp, ch2 (counts as first htr), 2htr in same sp, [3htr in next ch-2 sp] until half of circumference is joined. Place two mirrors between mandalas ensuring mirrors are facing out on both sides, [3htr in next ch-2 sp] to end enclosing mirror, ss in top of beg ch-2 to join. (*72 htr*)
Fasten off.
Thread 24 beads onto fifth colour to be used for round 5.
Round 5: Join fifth colour in any sp between 3-htr groups, *ch2, bring up bead, ch1, ss to 2nd ch from hook (working over bead), ch1, 1dc in next sp between 3-htr groups; rep from * to end, ss in first ch of beg ch-2 to join.
Fasten off.

Ball

(make 1 for each tassel)
Using any colour make magic ring, leaving a 10cm (4in) tail.
Round 1: Ch1 (does not count as a st), 5dc into ring. (*5 dc*)
Work in a continuous spiral. PM in last st and move up as each round is finished.
Round 2: 2dc in each st to end. (*10 dc*)
Round 3: 1dc in each st to end.
Round 4: [Dc2tog] twice, stuff ball with yarn tail, [dc2tog] 3 times. (*5 dc*)
Fasten off, sew in end around top to close.

Making up and finishing

Using any colour, make a tassel (see page 125).
Thread 3 glass beads onto the tassel tie at the top, followed by the crochet ball, and then tie onto the mandala through round 5. Sew in securely.

Count 12 beads around from where the tassel is joined and place a marker in the space; this is where the key ring fixing will be joined.
Join any colour around the D-ring of the key ring fixing and work 4dc around the ring, work 2dc into the sp marked with the marker to join the fixing to the mandala, then cont with 4dc around the ring.
Fasten off.
Sew in ends.

Zipped Make-up Bags

There are many ways to enjoy colours and how they relate to each other, and in this project I've devised two different ones: the larger bag has a stripe in a cooler shade, which accentuates the hotter colours, while the smaller bag has colours chosen purely at random to explore their interaction.

Skill level: **

YARN AND MATERIALS

Rico Ricorumi DK (100% cotton, approx. 57m/62yd per 25g/⅞oz ball) DK (light worsted) weight yarn:

 1 ball each of:
 Orange shade 027 (A)
 Berry shade 015 (B)
 Orchid shade 016 (C)
 Raspberry shade 013 (D)
 Light Green shade 046 (E)
 Fuchsia shade 014 (F)
 Lilac shade 017 (G)
 Red shade 028 (H)
 Purple shade 020 (I)
 Sky Blue shade 031 (J)
 Emerald shade 042 (K)

16cm (6½in) zip (large bag)

12cm (5in) zip (small bag)

HOOKS AND EQUIPMENT

3mm (US size C/2–D/3) crochet hook

Yarn needle

Stitch marker

FINISHED MEASUREMENTS

Large bag: 11cm (4¼in) deep x 18cm (7in) wide at top x 10cm (4in) diameter at base

Small bag: 9cm (3½in) deep x 14cm (5½in) wide at top x 9cm (3½in) diameter at base

TENSION

Rounds 1–3 of base measure 2.5cm (1in) diameter using a 3mm (US size C/2–D/3) hook.

ABBREVIATIONS

See page 127.

Large bag

Using A, make a magic ring.

Round 1: Ch1 (does not count as a st throughout), 6dc into ring, ss in first dc to join. (6 sts)

Round 2: Ch1, 2dc in same st at base of ch-1, 2dc in each st to end, ss in first dc to join. (12 sts)

Round 3: Ch1, 1dc in same st at base of ch-1, 2dc in next st, [1dc in next st, 2dc in next st] 5 times, ss in first dc to join. (18 sts)

Round 4: Ch1, 1dc in same st at base of ch-1, 1dc in next st, 2dc in next st, [1dc in each of next 2 sts, 2dc in next st] 5 times, ss in first dc to join. (24 sts)

Round 5: Ch1, 1dc in same st at base of ch-1, 1dc in each of next 2 sts, 2dc in next st, [1dc in each of next 3 sts, 2dc in next st] 5 times, ss in first dc to join. (30 sts)

Colour combinations

LARGE BAG

For the large bag work rounds 1–13 in same colour throughout.

SMALL BAG

For the base of the smaller bag change colour for each round. When working the sides in a continuous spiral, change colour as and when – usually several times each round.

COLOUR THERAPY

A cooler colour will temper the hot reds and oranges used on the larger bag – I've used lime, but you could experiment with emerald green or sky blue instead.

When working the smaller bag, play lucky dip by picking colours at random – enjoy seeing how the colours interact as you work the sides, changing colour as frequently as you like.

Rounds 6–12: Cont to inc 6 sts evenly per round in patt as set. (*72 sts*)
Round 13: Ch1, working in BLO for this round, 1dc BLO in each st to end, ss in first dc to join.

SIDES
Round 14: Ch1, 1dc in each st to end, ss in first dc to join.
Changing yarn colour on last yrh of ss at end of round, rep round 14 while working colour sequence as foll:
Rounds 15–16: Yarn A.
Rounds 17–18: Yarn B.
Rounds 19–21: Yarn C.
Rounds 22–23: Yarn D.
Rounds 24–26: Yarn E.
Rounds 27–28: Yarn F.
Rounds 29–31: Yarn B.
Rounds 32–33: Yarn G.
Rounds 34–36: Yarn A.
Round 39: With RS still facing and cont in A, working from left to right, work backward (crab stitch – working backward from left to right for right-handed crochet, reverse if working left-handed) working 1dc in each st around.
Fasten off.

Small bag
Using any colour, make a magic ring. Changing colour every round, work rounds 1–10 as for large bag. (*60 sts*)
Round 11: Ch1, working in BLO for this round, 1dc BLO in each st to end, ss in first dc to join.

SIDES
PM to denote end of round and move up as each round is complete. Work in a continuous spiral, changing colour at least twice per round.
Rounds 12–29: 1dc in each st to end.
Round 30: With RS still facing, working from left to right, work backward (crab stitch) working 1dc in each st around.
Fasten off.

Making up and finishing
Sew in ends.
Pin one side of zip to one side of top opening inside bag, and sew in place. Pin other side of zip to match on other side of opening and tuck in spare tape at each end. Open zip and sew other side, making extra stitches at each end to keep tape ends tucked away. Rep on second bag.

Summer Love Wall Hanging

This wall hanging has to be one of my favourite pieces because of the joyous colours, which have a welcoming vibrancy that lifts my heart – you may have noticed my tendency to lean toward this palette. Interestingly, as I sewed the little shisha mirrors onto the squares, I had an urge to flip the colours and work the same piece a second time in the more calming blues and greens.

Skill level: *

YARN AND MATERIALS

Rico Ricorumi DK (100% cotton, approx. 57m/62yd per 25g/⅞oz ball) DK (light worsted) weight yarn:
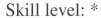
1 ball each of:
Tangerine shade 026 (A)
Orange shade 027 (B)
Red shade 028 (C)
Wine Red shade 029 (D)
Sky Blue shade 031 (E)
Raspberry shade 013 (F)
Fuchsia shade 014 (G)
Berry shade 015 (H)
Purple shade 020 (I)
Candy Pink shade 012 (J)
Emerald shade 042 (K)
Grass Green shade 044 (L)

Scheepjes Maxi Sweet Treat (100% mercerised cotton, approx. 140m/153yd per 25g/⅞oz ball) 2-ply (lace) weight yarn:
1 ball each of:
Electric Blue shade 201 (M)
Jade shade 514 (N)
Tangerine shade 281 (O)
Yellow Gold shade 208 (P)
Vivid Blue shade 146 (Q)

13 shisha mirrors approx. 16mm (⅝in) diameter

43cm (17in) length of dowling

HOOKS AND EQUIPMENT

3mm (US size C/2–D/3) crochet hook

Yarn needle

FINISHED MEASUREMENTS

43cm (17in) wide x 37cm (14½in) long excluding tassels

45cm (17¾in) long with tassels

TENSION

Rounds 1–3 of square measure 5cm (2in) diameter using a 3mm (US size C/2–D/3) hook.

ABBREVIATIONS

See page 127.

Squares

(make 36)
Using any colour, make a magic ring.
Round 1: Ch3 (counts as first tr), (2tr, ch1) into ring, [3tr, ch1] 3 times into ring, ss in top of beg ch-3 to join. (*12tr + 4 ch-1 sps*)
Fasten off first colour.
Round 2: Join second colour in any ch-1 sp, ch2 (counts as first htr), (1htr, ch2, 2htr) in same sp (first corner made), *1htr in each of next 3 sts, (2htr, ch2, 2htr) in next ch-1 sp (corner made); rep from * twice more, 1htr in each of next 3 sts, ss in top of beg ch-2 to join. (*28htr + 4 ch-2 sps*)
Fasten off second colour.
Round 3: Join third colour in any ch-2 sp, ch3 (counts as first dc and ch2), 1dc in same sp, *1dc in each of next 7 sts, (1dc, ch2, 1dc) in corner sp; rep from * twice more, 1dc in each of next 7 sts, ss in first ch of beg ch-3 to join. (*36dc + 4 ch-2 sps*)
Fasten off, leaving a 15cm (6in) tail.

Triangles

(make 4)
Using any colour, make a magic ring.
Row 1: Ch3 (counts as first tr), (3tr, ch1, 4tr) into ring, changing colour on last yarn round hook, turn. (*8tr + 1 ch-1 sp*)
Row 2: Ch2 (counts as first htr), 2htr in first st, 1htr in each of next 3 sts, (2htr, ch2, 2htr) in next ch-1 sp (corner made), 1htr in each of next 3 sts, 3htr in last st (top of beg ch-3), changing colour on last yarn round hook, turn. (*16htr + 1 ch-2 sp*)

Row 3: Ch1 (does not count as a st), miss first st, 2dc in next st, 1dc in each of next 6 sts, (1dc, ch2, 1dc) in ch-2 corner sp, 1dc in each of next 6 sts, 2dc in next st, do not turn. Cont round with (ch2, 1dc) in same st (second corner made), work 7dc evenly along edge, 1dc in same st as beg 2-dc, ch2, ss in first dc to join.
Fasten off.

Shisha mirror frames

(make 13)
Using M, N, O, P or Q, make a magic ring. Ch2 (counts as first htr), 23htr into ring, ss in top of beg ch-2 to join.
Fasten off and pull tail to close loop slightly allowing a small hole for shisha mirror to peek through.

Making up and finishing

Arrange the squares and triangles in any order to create the heart shape, following the photograph on page 40 as a guide. Using the tail ends of the squares, sew squares together by holding two squares with RS together, aligning corners, and sewing through the back loops of the edge stitches to join. Add the triangles in the same way, to fill in around the edge and complete the heart shape.

Sew the shisha mirror frames to the points where four squares join, using the photograph as a guide, and sliding the shisha mirror into the frame before completing the seam.

TASSELS
Cut 25cm (10in) lengths of 5 colours to make 25 tassels (see page 125). Add one tassel at the join between squares and in the middle of each square along the bottom edge. Finish by trimming the tassels to one equal length.

HANGING LOOPS
Using any Ricorumi colour, join yarn in any ch-2 corner sp of the top triangles, ch12, ss to first chain to join.
Fasten off and sew in ends.
Repeat for each top corner ch-2 sp to create 4 hanging loops in total.

Mandala Cushion

I love the glow that is generated whenever pink and orange are placed together and I never tire of twinning these colours in all their shades. This has to be my happiest palette – to which my Instagram feed will testify! This pattern is fairly open in places, so you will need a plain white cover on the cushion beneath for it to look its best.

Skill level: ***

YARN AND MATERIALS

Rico Creative Cotton Aran (100% cotton, approx. 85m/93yd per 50g/1¾oz ball) aran (worsted) weight yarn:

    1 ball each of:
    Tangerine shade 76 (A)
    Nature shade 60 (B)
    Rose shade 00 (C)
    Candy Pink shade 64 (D)
    Fuchsia shade 13 (E)

Rico Creative Lamé DK (62% polyester, 28% polyamide, 130m/142yd per 25g/⅞oz ball) DK (light worsted) weight yarn:
    1 ball of Gold shade 002 (F)

45cm (18in) diameter cushion with plain white cover

HOOKS AND EQUIPMENT

4mm (US size G/6) crochet hook

Yarn needle

Sewing needle and white thread to sew crochet to cushion

FINISHED MEASUREMENTS

47cm (18½in) diameter

TENSION

Rounds 1 and 2 measure 4cm (1½in) diameter using a 4mm (US size G/6) hook.

ABBREVIATIONS

See page 127.

SPECIAL ABBREVIATIONS

2trCL (2-treble cluster): [yarn round hook, insert hook in stitch, yarn round hook, pull through the work, yarn round hook, pull through two loops on the hook] twice in same stitch, yarn round hook and pull through all loops on hook to complete cluster

tr4tog (treble crochet 4 stitches together): [yarn round hook, insert hook in next stitch, yarn round hook, pull through the work, yarn round hook, pull through two loops on the hook] 4 times, yarn round hook and pull through all loops on hook to complete stitch

tr7tog (treble crochet 7 stitches together): [yarn round hook, insert hook in next stitch, yarn round hook, pull through the work, yarn round hook, pull through two loops on the hook] 7 times, yarn round hook and pull through all loops on hook to complete stitch

4trPC (4-treble popcorn): inserting hook in same stitch each time, work 4 complete trebles, slip hook out of last loop on hook and insert it into top of first stitch, then insert hook back into loop of last stitch again, yarn round hook, pull through loop on hook and first stitch to join and complete popcorn

edtr (extended double treble): work a double treble stitch in the next ch-1 space two rows below

FPdc (front post double crochet): insert hook from front to back to front around post of stitch in row below, yarn round hook, draw yarn around post of stitch, yarn round hook and pull through both loops on hook

FPhtr (front post half treble): working from the front, yarn round hook, insert hook from front to back to front around post of stitch in row below, yarn round hook, draw yarn around post of stitch (3 loops on hook), yarn round hook, pull through all 3 loops on hook

FPtr (front post treble): working from the front, yarn round hook, insert hook from front to back to front around post of stitch in row below, yarn round hook, draw yarn around post of stitch, [yarn round hook, pull through 2 loops] twice

MFPB (make front post bobble): *yarn round hook, insert hook from front to back to front around post of extended double treble 2 rows below, yarn round hook, draw yarn around post of stitch, yarn round hook, pull yarn through first 2 loops on hook; rep from * 3 more times around same post, yarn round hook, pull through all loops on hook

Cushion front

Using A, make a magic ring.

Round 1: Ch1 (does not count as a st), 8dc into ring, ss in first dc to join. (*8 sts*)
Fasten off A.

Round 2: Join B in any st, ch3 (counts as first tr), 1tr in same st, 2tr in each st to end, ss in top of beg ch-3 to join. (*16 sts*)
Fasten off B.

Round 3: Working in BLO, join D in any back loop, ch3 changing to C on last yrh (counts as first tr), 1FPtr in same st working around tr post from round 2, change to D, *1tr BLO in next st, change to C, 1FPtr in same st working around tr post from round 2, change to D; rep from * to end, ss in top of beg ch-3 to join.
Fasten off C and D. (*16 tr + 16 FPtr*)

Round 4: Join A in BLO of any tr st, ch3 (counts as first tr), 1tr BLO in same st, change to D, 1FPtr around post of next FPtr from round 3, change to A, *2tr BLO in next tr, change to D, 1FPtr around next FPtr from round 3, change to A; rep from * to end, ss in top of beg ch-3 to join. (*16 FPtr + 32 tr*)
Fasten off A and D.

Round 5: Join F in BLO of any st to left of a FPtr, ch1 (counts as first dc), 1dc BLO in next st, 1FPhtr around FPtr from round 4, *1dc BLO in each of next 2 sts, 1FPhtr around next FPtr; rep from * to end, ss in beg ch-1 to join. (*16 FPhtr + 32 dc*)
Fasten off F.

Round 6: Join B in any dc to left of a FPhtr, ch1 (counts as first dc), 1dc in next st, 1dc in FPhtr, ch1, *1dc in each of next 2 sts, 1dc in FPhtr, ch1; rep from * 15 times, ss in beg ch-1 to join. (*48 dc + 16 ch-1 sps*)

Round 7: Join D in any st to left of a ch-1 sp, ch2 (counts as first tr in tr7tog), [yrh, insert hook in next st, yrh, pull through the work, yrh, pull through two loops on hook] 6 times (counting ch-1 sp as a st), yrh, pull through all loops on hook (first tr7tog complete), ch9, miss ch-1 sp, *tr7tog across next 7 sts (counting ch-1 sp as a st), ch9, miss ch-1 sp; rep from * to end, ss in top of first tr7tog to join.
Fasten off D.

Round 8: Join B in any ch-9 sp, ch1 (counts as first dc), 2dc in same sp, 1edtr in ch-1 sp from round 6, 3dc in same ch-9 sp, 1FPdc around top of tr7tog, *3dc in next ch-9 sp, 1edtr in ch-1 sp from round 6, 3dc in same ch-9 sp, 1FPdc around top of tr7tog; rep from * to end, ss in beg ch-1 to join. (*56 dc + 8 edtr*)
Fasten off B.

Round 9: Join C in any dc to left of edtr in round 8, ch1 (counts as first dc), 1dc in each of next 7 sts, ch1, *1dc in each of next 8 sts, ch1; rep from * to end, ss in beg ch-1 to join. (*64 dc + 8 ch-1 sps*)
Fasten off C.

Round 10: Join E in any ch-1 sp, ch1 (counts as first dc), 1dc in each of next 8 sts, change to A, MFPB around edtr from round 8, change to E, *1dc in next ch-1 sp, 1dc in each of next 8 sts, change to A, MFPB around edtr from round 8, change to E; rep from * to end, ss in beg ch-1 to join.
Fasten off E and A.

Round 11: Join D in any st to left of MFPB, ch2 (counts as first htr), 1htr in each of next 8 sts, 1FPhtr around top of MFPB, *1htr in each of next 9 sts, 1FPhtr around top of MFPB; rep from * to end, ss in top of beg ch-2 to join. (*80 sts*)

Round 12: Join F in any st to left of FPhtr, ch1 (counts as first dc), 1dc in each of next 8 sts, 1dc in FPhtr, 1FPdc around same FPhtr (first inc made), *1dc in each of next 9 sts, 1dc in FPhtr, 1FPdc around same FPhtr; rep from * to end, ss in beg ch-1 to join. (*88 sts*)
Fasten off F.

Round 13: Join C in any FPdc, ch3 (counts as first tr), 1tr in same st, *1tr in each of next 5 sts, change to E, 4trPC, change to C, 1tr in each of next 4 sts, 2tr in next st; rep from * to end omitting final 2tr on last rep, ss in top of beg ch-3 to join. (*96 sts*)

Round 14: Join F in top of any 4trPC, ch1 (counts as first dc), 1dc in same st (first inc made), 1dc in each of next 11 sts, *2dc in next st, 1dc in each of next 11 sts; rep from * to end, ss in beg ch-1 to join. (*104 sts*)
Fasten off F.

Round 15: Join A in second of any 2-dc inc from prev round, ch1 (counts as first dc), 1dc in same st (first inc made), 1dc in each of next 12 sts, *2dc in next st, 1dc in each of next 12 sts; rep from * to end, ss in beg ch-1 to join. (*112 sts*)
Fasten off A.

Round 16: Join B in second of any 2-dc inc from prev round, ch1 (counts as first dc), 1dc in same st (first inc made), 1dc in each of next 13 sts, *2dc in next st, 1dc in each of next 13 sts; rep from * to end, ss in beg ch-1 to join. (*120 sts*)
Fasten off B.

Round 17: Join D in second of any 2-dc inc from prev round, ch2 (counts as first htr), 1htr in same st (first inc made), 1htr in each of next 14 sts, *2htr in next st, 1htr in each of next 14 sts; rep from * to end, ss in top of beg ch-2 to join. (*128 sts*)
Fasten off D.

Round 18: Join E in any st, ch3 (counts as first tr of 2trCL), yrh, insert hook in same st as ch-3, yrh, pull through the work, yrh, pull through all loops on hook (first 2trCL complete), ch3, 2trCL in same st, *miss next 3 sts, (2trCL, ch3, 2trCL) in next st; rep from * to end, ss in top of beg 2trCL to join. (*64 2-trCl + 32 ch-3 sps*)
Fasten off E.

Round 19: Join C in any ch-3 sp, ch1 (counts as first dc), 3dc in same sp, change to F, 1dc in sp between next two 2trCL, change to C, 4dc in next 3-ch sp, change to F, 1dc in sp between next two 2trCL; rep from * to end, ss in beg ch-1 to join. (*160 sts*) Fasten off C and F.

Round 20: Join A in dc to left of any dc in F, ch2 (counts as first tr in tr4tog), [yrh, insert hook in next st, yrh, pull through the work, yrh, pull through 2 loops on hook] 3 times, yrh, pull through all loops on hook (first tr4tog complete), ch6, miss next dc in F, *tr4tog across next 4 sts, ch6, miss next dc in F; rep from * to end, ss in top of first tr4tog to join. Fasten off A.

Round 21: Join B in any ch-6 sp, ch2 (counts as first htr), 4htr in same sp, change to F, 1FPtr around top of tr4tog, change to B, *5htr in next ch-6 sp, change to F, 1FPtr around top of tr4tog, change to B; rep from * to end, ss in top of beg ch-2 to join. (*192 sts*) Fasten off B and F.

Round 22: Join D in any FPtr, ch4 (counts as first tr and ch-1 sp), 1tr in same st, ch1, miss next st, [1tr, ch1, miss next st] 11 times, *(1tr, ch1, 1tr) in next st, ch1, miss next st, [1tr, ch1, miss next st] 11 times; rep from * to end, ss in third of beg ch-4 to join. (*104 sts + 104 ch-1 sps*) Fasten off D.

Round 23: Join F in any ch-1 sp, ch2 (counts as first dc and ch-1 sp), 1dc in next ch-1 sp, *ch1, 1dc in next ch-1 sp; rep from * to end, ch1, ss in first of beg ch-2 to join. Fasten off F.

Round 24: Join E in any ch-1 sp, ch3 (counts as first tr), 1tr in same ch-1 sp, *2tr in next ch-1 sp; rep from * to end, ss in top of beg ch-3 to join. (*208 sts*) Fasten off E.

Round 25: Join A in any sp between 2-tr groups, ch3 (counts as first tr), 1tr in same sp, *miss next 2 sts, 2tr in next sp between 2-tr groups; rep from * to end, ss in top of beg ch-3 to join. Fasten off A.

Round 26: Join B in any sp between 2-tr groups, ch5 (counts as first dc and ch-4 sp), miss next 4 sts, *1dc in next sp between 2-tr groups, ch4, miss next 4 sts; rep from * to end, ss in first of beg ch-5 to join. (*52 dc + 52 ch-4 sps*) Fasten off B.

Round 27: Join C in any ch-4 sp, ch1 (counts as first dc), (1htr, 1tr, 1htr, 1dc) all in same sp, *(1dc, 1htr, 1tr, 1htr, 1dc) in next ch-4 sp; rep from * to end, ss in beg ch-1 to join. Fasten off.

Making up and finishing

Sew in all ends.

Using a sewing needle threaded with white thread, sew the crochet piece to one side of cotton cushion cover all around the outer edge.

Tips

• Count your stitches every round especially at the beginning as it is so easy to miscount… I did… twice!

• When working two colours on the same round, change colour on last yarn round hook of current colour.

COLOUR THERAPY

The combination of pink and orange is my go-to colour choice whenever I need a little boost, whilst the warm yellow and tangerine orange give a rich sunshine feel that always lifts my spirits. White punctuates this pattern and offers definition to some of the rounds, with gold adding depth and sparkle resulting in a joyous burst of happiness.

chapter 3

Autumn

Woodland Walk Shoulder Bag

What an absolute feast for the senses this bag is! Inspired by the early signs of autumn, as the leaves begin their transition from green to brown, I have tried to capture the way the colours in every leaf blend together so beautifully, moving seamlessly from earthy green to pale yellow.

Skill level: **

YARN AND MATERIALS

Rico Ricorumi DK (100% cotton, 57m/62yd per 25g/⅞oz ball) DK (light worsted) weight yarn:
  1 ball each of:
  Teal shade 040 (A)
  Aqua shade 074 (B)
  Mauve shade 019 (C)
  Lavender shade 072 (D)
  Terracotta shade 069 (E)
  Lotus shade 067 (F)
  Apricot shade 070 (G)
  Saffron shade 063 (H)
  Pastel Yellow shade 062 (I)

Rico Ricorumi Lamé DK (62% polyester, 28% polyamide, 50m/54yd per 10g/⅓oz ball) DK (light worsted) weight yarn:
  1 ball of Gold shade 002 (J)

HOOKS AND EQUIPMENT

3.5mm (US size E/4) crochet hook

Stitch marker

Yarn needle

FINISHED MEASUREMENTS

Bag (not including strap): 20cm (8in) wide x 18cm (7¼in) deep
Strap: approx. 112cm (44in) long

TENSION

11 sts x 15 rows measures approx. 7cm (2¾in) square working pattern in round 4 using a 3.5mm (US size E/4) hook.

ABBREVIATIONS

See page 127.

SPECIAL ABBREVIATION

edc (extended double crochet): work a double crochet stitch in the next dc two rounds below

Bag

Foundation chain: Using A and B held together, ch31.
Round 1: 1dc in second ch from hook, 1dc in each of next 28 ch, 3dc in last ch, working back along other side of ch, 1dc in each st to last st, 3dc in last st, ss in beg dc to join. (*64 dc*)
Beg working in a continuous spiral, using st marker to mark beg of each round.
Round 2: 1dc in first st, PM, 1dc in each st to end, do not ss to join.
Round 3: Miss st with marker, 1dc in next st, PM, *1edc in next st, 1dc in next st; rep from * around ending with 1edc over st with marker (remove marker).
As corners begin to curl up turn work outward/inside out so you are working with outside edge facing you – this is the RS.

Colour combinations

Rounds 1–4	A/B
Rounds 5–6	B/C
Round 7	A/B
Round 8	B/D
Round 9	C/D
Round 10	D/B
Rounds 11–12	C/D
Round 13	C/E
Rounds 14–15	C/D
Round 16	D/E
Round 17	C/D
Rounds 18–19	D/E
Round 20	E/F
Round 21	D/E
Rounds 22–23	E/F
Round 24	F/G
Rounds 25–26	E/F
Rounds 27–28	F/G
Round 29	E/F
Rounds 30–31	F/G
Round 32	G/H
Round 33	F/G
Rounds 34–35	G/H
Rounds 36–38	H/I

Round 4: 1dc in next st (edc from prev round), PM, *1edc in next st, 1dc in next st; rep from * around ending with 1edc over st with marker (remove marker).

Rounds 5–37: Rep round 4, changing single strands of yarn at end of round as shown in colour combinations, ending round 37 with 1dc in beg dc of previous round.

Round 38: With RS still facing, working from left to right, work backward (crab stitch) working 1dc in each st around.

Fasten off.

Leaves

(make 12 in J, 2 in A and 2 in B)
Ch7, ss in second ch from hook, 1dc in next ch, 1tr in next ch, 1dtr in next ch, 1tr in next ch, 1dc in last ch.
Fasten off.

Berries

(make 6 in any colour and 2 in J)
Ch2, 5dc in first ch, 5dc in next ch.
Fasten off.

Strap

Using A and B held together as one strand, join yarn to top edge at one side of bag, ch150 (or adjust to suit) and join to opposite side top edge, 1dc in next st of top edge of bag.
Turn and ensure ch is not twisted.
Work 1dc in each ch to end, 1dc in st next to beg of strap to join to bag, ensuring strap is not twisted.
Fasten off and sew in ends to secure.

Making up and finishing

Sew one leaf in A and one in B where the strap joins the bag. Sew a gold berry where the two leaves meet at the top. Repeat on the other end of the strap.
Sew three pairs of gold leaves evenly spaced along the top of each side of the bag, placing a coloured berry where the two leaves meet and sewing them in position.

Tips

• Holding two strands together to make one strand throughout makes this bag strong and sturdy whilst also creating a beautiful blend of colours.

• Keep your tension tight to create a bag that has a solid structure.

Patchwork Gloves

The beautiful texture of this yarn enhances the interplay of colours, giving a real depth to these gloves. They are easier to construct than normal gloves – first you'll create the mini squares separately, then join them to create the gloves, and finally add the cuffs and finger edging.

Skill level: **

YARN AND MATERIALS
Rowan Felted Tweed DK (50% wool, 25% viscose, 25% alpaca, approx. 175m/191yd per 50g/1¾oz ball) DK (light worsted) weight yarn:
  1 ball each of:
  Tawny shade 186 (A)
  Seafarer shade 170 (B)
  Frozen shade 185
  Cinnamon shade 175
  Pink Bliss shade 199
  Avocado shade 161
  Mineral shade 181
  Zinnia shade 198
  Maritime shade 167

HOOKS AND EQUIPMENT
3.75mm (US size F/5) crochet hook

Yarn needle

FINISHED MEASUREMENTS
23cm (9in) long x 11cm (4¼in) wide

TENSION
Rounds 1 and 2 of mini square measure 3.5cm (1⅜in) square using a 3.75mm (US size F/5) hook.

ABBREVIATIONS
See page 127.

SPECIAL ABBREVIATIONS
BPhtr (back post half treble): working from the back, yarn round hook, insert hook from back to front to back around post of stitch in row below, yarn round hook, draw yarn around post of stitch (3 loops on hook), yarn round hook, pull through all 3 loops on hook
FPhtr (front post half treble): working from the front, yarn round hook, insert hook from front to back to front around post of stitch in row below, yarn round hook, draw yarn around post of stitch (3 loops on hook), yarn round hook, pull through all 3 loops on hook

Mini squares
(make 30 for each glove)
Using any colour, make a magic ring.
Round 1: Ch3 (counts as first tr), 11tr into ring, ss in top of beg ch-3 to join. (*12 tr*)
Fasten off first colour.
Round 2: Join second colour in any st, ch4 (counts as first htr and ch-2 sp), 1htr in same st (first corner made), *[1dc in next st] twice, (1htr, ch2, 1htr) in next st (second corner made); rep from * twice, 1dc in each of last 2 sts, ss in 2nd ch of beg ch-4 to join.
Fasten off.

> ### Tip
> • Leave a long tail after finishing each mini square to use for sewing the squares together later.

Making up and finishing

Arrange 30 mini squares into one large piece of 6 by 5 squares.

JOIN SQUARES

Hold 2 mini squares together with RS together. Align the corners and sew the squares together from one corner to the next corner, sewing through the back loops only. Repeat to join all 30 squares.

Lie flat with the 6 mini squares lying horizontally and the 5 rows vertically. Fold in half lengthways, so each half is 3 squares wide and 5 squares long. With RS together sew along the seam until the bottom two and a half squares have been joined together to make the wrist. Fasten off. Starting at the opposite end of seam, sew along the seam until one square has been joined at the top. Fasten off, leaving an opening of approximately one and a half squares for the thumb.

Repeat with the other 30 squares to make the second glove.

WRIST EDGING

Join B in first ch-2 corner sp of any mini square at wrist end.

Round 1: Ch1 (counts as first dc), miss first htr, 1dc in each of next 3 sts, 1dc in last ch-2 corner sp of mini square, *1dc in ch-2 corner sp of next mini square, miss next htr, 1dc in each of next 3 sts, 1dc in last ch-2 corner sp of mini square; rep from * 4 more times, ss in beg ch-1 to join. (30 dc)

Round 2: Ch2 (does not count as a st throughout), 1htr in each st to end, ss in first htr to join. (30 htr)

Rounds 3–5: Ch2, [1FPhtr in next st, 1BPhtr in next st] to end, ss in first FPhtr to join.
Fasten off.

FINGERS EDGING

Join B in first ch-2 corner sp of any mini square at fingers end.

Round 1: Ch1 (counts as first dc), miss first htr, 1dc in each of next 3 sts, 1dc in last ch-2 corner sp of mini square, *1dc in ch-2 corner sp of next mini square, miss first htr, 1dc in each of next 3 sts, 1dc in last ch-2 corner sp of mini square; rep from * 4 more times, ss in top of beg ch-1 to join. (30 dc)

Round 2: Ch2 (does not count as a st throughout), 1htr in each st to end, ss in first htr to join. (30 htr)

Round 3: Ch2, [1FPhtr in next st, 1BPhtr in next st] to end, ss in first FPhtr to join.
Fasten off B.

Round 4: Join A in any st, ch1 (does not count as a st), 1dc in each st to end, ss in first dc to join. (30 dc)
Fasten off.

THUMBHOLE EDGING

Join B in any st around thumbhole opening.

Round 1: Ch1 (counts as first dc throughout), 1dc in each st and corner ch sp around, ss in beg ch-1 to join. (approx. 18 dc, depending on size of opening)

Round 2: Ch1, 1dc in each st around, ss in beg ch-1 to join.
Fasten off.

Sew in all ends.

Dingle Dangle Garland

Sometimes the nature of the yarn determines the overall feel, no matter the colour. The soft texture of the yarn and the muted tones of oranges and pinks set against the rich burgundy and turquoise make this garland good enough to eat.

Skill level: **

YARN AND MATERIALS
Rowan Felted Tweed DK (50% wool, 25% viscose, 25% alpaca, approx. 175m/191yd per 50g/1¾oz ball) DK (light worsted) weight yarn:
  1 ball each of:
  Tawny shade 186 (A)
  Frozen shade 185 (B)
  Vaseline Green shade 204 (C)
  Turquoise shade 202 (D)
  Barbara shade 200 (E)
  Iris shade 201 (F)
  Zinnia shade 198 (G)
  Mineral shade 181 (H)
  Clay shade 177 (I)

Rico Ricorumi DK (100% cotton, 57m/62yd per 25g/⅞oz ball) DK (light worsted) weight yarn:
  Approx. 127cm (50in) length of
  Light Brown shade 052 (J)

Fibrefill toy stuffing

HOOKS AND EQUIPMENT
3.75mm (US size F/5) crochet hook
Yarn needle

FINISHED MEASUREMENTS
Finished garland: 114cm (45in) long
Large motif bauble: 10cm (4in) diameter
Mini motif bauble: 5cm (2in) diameter

TENSION
Rounds 1 and 2 of mini motif measure 3.5cm (1⅜in) diameter using a 3.75mm (US size F/5) hook.

ABBREVIATIONS
See page 127.

SPECIAL ABBREVIATION
edc (extended double crochet): work a double crochet stitch in the next dc two rounds below

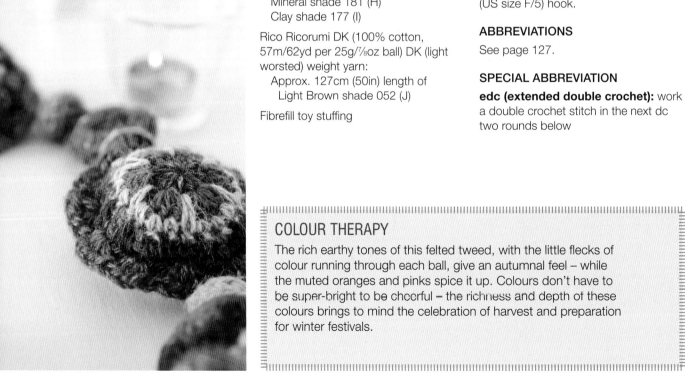

COLOUR THERAPY
The rich earthy tones of this felted tweed, with the little flecks of colour running through each ball, give an autumnal feel – while the muted oranges and pinks spice it up. Colours don't have to be super-bright to be cheerful – the richness and depth of these colours brings to mind the celebration of harvest and preparation for winter festivals.

Colour combinations

LARGE MOTIF BAUBLE 1

Round 1	Yarn H
Round 2	Yarn I
Round 3	Yarn A
Rounds 4 and 6	Yarn F
Round 5	Yarn E

LARGE MOTIF BAUBLE 2

Round 1	Yarn E
Round 2	Yarn D
Round 3	Yarn B
Rounds 4 and 6	Yarn G
Round 5	Yarn A

LARGE MOTIF BAUBLE 3

Round 1	Yarn I
Round 2	Yarn F
Round 3	Yarn G
Rounds 4 and 6	Yarn C
Round 5	Yarn H

LARGE MOTIF BAUBLE 4

Round 1	Yarn A
Round 2	Yarn B
Round 3	Yarn C
Rounds 4 and 6	Yarn E
Round 5	Yarn D

LARGE MOTIF BAUBLE 5

Round 1	Yarn D
Round 2	Yarn C
Round 3	Yarn E
Rounds 4 and 6	Yarn H
Round 5	Yarn G

LARGE MOTIF BAUBLE 6

Round 1	Yarn F
Round 2	Yarn E
Round 3	Yarn H
Rounds 4 and 6	Yarn A
Round 5	Yarn I

Large motif bauble

(make 2 in each colour combination)
Using first colour, make a magic ring.
Round 1: Ch2 (counts as first htr), 11htr into ring, ss in top of beg ch-2 to join. (*12 htr*)
Fasten off first colour.
Round 2: Join second colour in any st, ch2 (counts as first htr), 2htr in same st, ch1, miss next st, [3htr in next st, ch1, miss next st] 5 times, ss in top of beg ch-2 to join. (*Six 3-tr groups*)
Fasten off second colour.
Round 3: Join third colour in any missed st from round 2, bring yarn up to level of round 2 and ch1 (counts as first edc), [1dc in each of next 3 sts, 1edc in next missed st from round 1] 5 times, 1dc in each of next 3 sts, ss in top of beg long ch-1 to join. (*24 sts*)
Fasten off third colour.
Round 4: Join fourth colour in any st, ch3 (counts as first dc and ch-2 sp), miss next st, [1dc, ch2, miss next st] 11 times, ss in top of beg ch-3 to join. (*12 dc + 12 ch-2 sps*)
Fasten off fourth colour.
Round 5: Join fifth colour in any ch-2 sp, ch1 (counts as first dc), 1edc in next missed dc from round 3, 1dc in same ch-2 sp as first dc, ch1, [working into next 2-ch sp: 1dc in ch-2 sp, 1edc in next missed dc from round 3, 1dc in same ch-2 sp, ch1] 11 times, ss in beg ch-1 to join.
Fasten off fifth colour.

JOIN MOTIFS
Hold two matching motifs with WS tog, aligning ch-1 sps in round 5 to enable you to work through ch-1 sps of both motifs throughout.
Round 6: Join fourth colour in any ch-1 sp, ch2 (counts as first htr), 4htr in same sp, [5htr in next ch-1 sp] 11 times, ss in top of beg ch-2 to join.
Fasten off fourth colour.
Rep to make 6 large baubles.

Mini motif bauble

(make 12)
Use any colour combination, changing colour for each round.
Using first colour, make a magic ring.
Round 1: Ch2 (counts as first htr throughout), 9htr into ring, ss in top of beg ch-2 to join. (*10 htr*)
Fasten off first colour.
Round 2: Join second colour in any st, ch2, 1htr in same st, 2htr in each st to end, ss in top of beg ch-2 to join. (*20 htr*)

Fasten off second colour.
Make second mini motif then hold with WS tog.
JOIN MOTIFS
Round 3: Working in BLO of both motifs tog, join third colour in any st, ch1 (counts as first dc), [2dc in next st, 1dc in next st] 7 times, stuff toy filling and all loose ends in sp between motifs, cont to close gap with [2dc in next st, 1dc in next st] twice, 2dc in next st, ss in beg ch-1 to join. (*30 dc*)
Join all 12 mini motifs to make 6 mini baubles.

Mini ball

(make 26 pieces, using any colours)
Using any colour and leaving a 20cm (8in) tail, make a magic ring.
Round 1: Ch3 (counts as first tr), 11tr into ring, ss in top of beg ch-3 to join. (*12 tr*)
Fasten off, leaving a 15cm (6in) end.

JOIN BALLS
Hold 2 mini ball pieces with WS tog, aligning sts. Sew together using long tail end of second side, working through FLO, stuffing all long ends into the middle to make it puff out.
Fasten off.
Rep to make 13 mini balls.

Making up and finishing

Cut approx. 120cm (48in) of the Ricorumi and make a double knot at the end. Thread the components onto it in the following order: 1 mini ball, 1 mini motif bauble, 1 mini ball, 1 large motif bauble. Repeat this sequence, ending with 1 mini ball.
Sew the end into the mini ball to secure it.

HANGING STRING
For added stability (as this yarn is very soft and can break easily), hold two strands of any yarn together to form one thread, join yarn to top of last mini ball and ch30, ss in 12th chain from hook to form a loop.
Fasten off.
Sew in ends.

Striped Purses

Sometimes the nature of the crochet stitches themselves can alter the way colours look. Notice how the textured surface of the texture striped purse blends the stripes slightly, bringing the colours together and making them interact with one another. This is in contrast to the smooth, even surface of the plain double crochet on the dotty striped purse, where the dots of colour are clearly defined.

Skill level: **

YARN AND MATERIALS

Scheepjes Cahlista Aran Cotton (100% natural cotton, approx. 26m/28yd per 15g/½oz ball) aran (worsted) weight yarn:

1 ball each of:
Shadow Purple shade 394 (A)
Ginger Gold shade 383 (B)
Soft Beige shade 406 (C)
Silver Blue shade 528 (D)
Rose Wine shade 396 (E)
Saffron shade 249 (F)
Camel shade 502 (G)
Deep Violet shade 521 (H)
Rust shade 388 (I)
English Tea shade 404 (J)

5 small wooden buttons, 12mm (½in) diameter

HOOKS AND EQUIPMENT

3mm (US size C/2–D/3) crochet hook

2 stitch markers

Yarn needle

FINISHED MEASUREMENTS

Dotty striped purse (closed): 12cm (4¾in) wide x 10cm (4in) deep

Texture striped purse (closed): 12cm (4¾in) wide x 9cm (3½in) deep

TENSION

11 sts x 13 rows measures 5cm (2in) square working double crochet using a 3mm (US size C/2–D/3) hook.

ABBREVIATIONS

See page 127.

Dotty striped purse

(make 2, yarn in brackets denotes colour for second purse)
Using A (B), ch29.
Round 1: 1dc in second ch from hook, 1dc in each of next 26 ch, 2dc in last ch, working along other side of ch, 1dc in each ch to end, ss in first dc to join. (*56 sts*)
Rounds 2–4: Ch1 (does not count as a st throughout), 1dc in same st at base of ch-1, 1dc in each st to end, ss in first dc to join.
Round 5: Ch1, 1dc in same st at base of ch-1, *change to C (D), 1dc in next st, change to A (B), 1dc in next st; rep from * to end, alternating colour on each st, ss in first dc to join, joining in next colour on last yarn round hook of round.
Fasten off both previous colours.
Rounds 6–9: Rep round 2 four times using E (F).
Round 10: Rep round 5 using E and G (F and H).
Rounds 11–14: Rep round 2 four times using I (G).
Round 15: Rep round 5 using I and A (G and E).
Rounds 16–19: Rep round 2 four times using B (C).
Round 20: Rep round 5 using B and C (C and B).
Rounds 21-24: Rep round 2 four times using F (J).
Round 25: Rep round 5 using F and I (J and F).

FLAP
Place marker in st at one side of purse opening, count 27 sts and place second marker in next st – you should have 2 markers evenly spaced with 27 sts between them.
Row 1 (RS): Join F (A) in first marked st, ch1 (does not count as a st), 1dc in same st at base of ch-1, 1dc in each st to next marker, 1dc in marked st, turn, remove markers. (*29 dc*)
Rows 2–6: Ch1 (does not count as a st throughout), 1dc in same st at base of ch-1, 1dc in each st to end. (*29 sts*)
Row 7: Ch1, miss first st, 1dc in each st to last 2 sts, dc2tog. (*27 sts*)
Rows 8–11: Rep row 7 four times. (*19 sts*)
Row 12: Ch1, 1dc in each of next 9 sts, ch3, miss next st, 1dc in each of next 9 sts. Fasten off.

Texture striped purse

(make 2, using any colour combination)
Foundation chain: Using any colour, ch23.
Round 1: 1dc in second ch from hook, 1dc in each of next 20 ch, 2dc in last ch, working along other side of ch, 1dc in each ch to end, ss in first dc to join. (*44 sts*)
Round 2: Ch1 (does not count as a st throughout), 1dc in same st at base of ch-1, *1tr in next st, 1dc in next st; rep from * to last st, 1tr in last st, ss in first dc to join.

Round 3: Ch1, 1tr in same st at base of ch-1, *1dc in next st, 1tr in next st; rep from * to last st, 1dc in last st, ss in first tr to join.
Round 4: Rep round 2.
Fasten off first colour.
Round 5: Join second colour, rep round 3.
Fasten off second colour.
Round 6: Join third colour, rep round 2.
Round 7: Rep round 3.
Round 8: Rep round 2.
Fasten off third colour.
Round 9: Join fourth colour, rep round 3.
Fasten off fourth colour.
Round 10: Join fifth colour, rep round 2.
Round 11: Rep round 3.
Round 12: Rep round 2.
Fasten off fifth colour.
Round 13: Join sixth colour, rep round 3.
Fasten off sixth colour.
Round 14: Join seventh colour, rep round 2.
Round 15: Rep round 3.
Round 16: Rep round 2.
Fasten off seventh colour.
Round 17: Join eighth colour, rep round 3.
Fasten off.

FLAP
Place marker in st at one side of purse opening, count 21 sts and place second marker in next st – you should have 2 markers evenly spaced with 21 sts between them. Keep markers in place as you will need them for row 11.
Row 1 (RS): Join yarn in first marked stitch, ch1 (does not count as a st), 1dc in same st at base of ch-1, 1dc in each st to next marker, 1dc in marked stitch, turn. (*23 dc*)
Rows 2–6: Ch1 (does not count as a st throughout), 1dc in same st at base of ch-1, 1dc in each st to end. (*23 sts*)

Row 7: Ch1, miss first st, 1dc in each st to last 2 sts, dc2tog. (*21 sts*)
Rows 8–10: Rep row 7 three times. (*15 sts*)
Fasten off.
Row 11: With RS of flap facing, join new colour in first marked st, remove marker, work 9dc up side of flap, 2dc in first st of row 10, 1dc in each of next 6 sts, ch3, miss next st, 1dc in each of next 6 sts, 2dc in last st, work 9dc down second side of flap, ss in second marked st, remove marker.
Fasten off and sew in ends.

Alternative texture striped purse

Work as for texture striped purse but change colour on round 4 to make first stripe, then work two rounds in next colour, followed by one round in next colour, to end.
Make flap as for texture striped purse.

Making up and finishing

Sew in ends.
Sew a button onto the front of each purse to match the chain fastening on the flap.

Season's End Scarf

This scarf reflects the change of seasons from autumn into winter, with its white snowflake centre and cool pale blue. The overall autumnal feel is preserved by the warmth of rich rusty red and deep burgundy hue. Obviously I chose bright pink as my border for this scarf because it's my default go-to colour, but you could choose to use whichever is your favourite from this palette.

Skill level: **

YARN AND MATERIALS

West Yorkshire Spinners The Croft Shetland Colours Aran (100% Shetland wool, approx. 166m/182yd per 100g/3½oz hank) aran (worsted) weight yarn:

1 ball each of:
Sullom shade 010 (A)
Melby shade 551 (B)
Norwick shade 172 (C)
Ollaberry shade 568 (D)
Fetlar shade 312 (E)
Belmont shade 554 (F)
Huxter shade 397 (G)
Voxter shade 099 (H)

HOOKS AND EQUIPMENT

5mm (US size H/8) crochet hook

Yarn needle

FINISHED MEASUREMENTS

192cm (75½in) long x 20cm (8in) wide

TENSION

Rounds 1 and 2 measure 6cm (2⅜in) diameter using a 5mm (US size H/8) hook.

ABBREVIATIONS

See page 127.

Foundation square

Using A, make a magic ring.

Round 1: Ch4 (counts as first tr and ch1), [1tr, ch1] 7 times into ring, ss in third ch of beg ch-4 to join. (*8 tr + 8 ch-1 sps*)
Fasten off A.

Round 2: Join any colour in any ch-1 sp, ch3 (counts as tr throughout), 2tr in same ch-1 sp, [3tr in next ch-1 sp] 7 times, ss in top of beg ch-3 to join. (*24 tr*)
Fasten off.

Round 3: Join next colour in any sp between 3-tr groups, ch2 (does not count as st), (1tr, ch3, tr2tog) in same sp, [miss next 3-tr, (tr2tog, ch3, tr2tog) in next sp between 3-tr groups] 7 times, miss next 3-tr and beg ch-2, ss in first tr to join.
Fasten off.

Round 4: Join next colour in any ch-3 sp, ch1 (counts as first dc), 4dc in same ch-3 sp, 1dc in sp between tr2tog, [5dc in next ch-5 sp, 1dc in sp between tr2tog] 7 times, ss in beg ch-1 to join. (*48 sts*)
Fasten off.

Round 5: Join next colour in any single dc that sits in the joining sp between tr2tog (not one of the 5-dc), ch3, (2tr, ch2, 3tr) in same st (first corner made), *[miss next 2 sts, (1dc, ch1, 1dc) in next st] 3 times, miss next 2 sts, (3tr, ch2, 3tr) in next st; rep from * twice more, [miss next 2 sts, (1dc, ch1, 1dc) in next st] 3 times, ss in top of beg ch-3 to join.
Fasten off.

Round 6: Join H in any ch-2 corner sp, ch3, (2tr, ch2, 3tr) in same sp (first corner made), *miss next 4 sts, [(1tr, ch2, 1tr) in ch-1 sp, miss next 2 sts] 3 times, miss next 4 sts, (3tr, ch2, 3tr) in ch-3 corner sp (next corner made); rep from * twice more, miss next 4 sts, [(1tr, ch2, 1tr) in ch-1 sp, miss next 2 sts] 3 times, ss in top of beg ch-3 to join.
Fasten off.

Current square

(make 11)
Work as for foundation square to end of round 5.

JOIN SQUARES
Beg working join-as-you-go (see page 126) on round 6 to join squares tog.

Round 6: Work first side of current square including first 3-tr group of corner, then instead of making ch-2 for corner sp, insert hook in corner sp of previous square, 1dc in corner sp of previous square (counts as first of 2-ch for corner sp), ch1, then work second 3-tr group in corner sp of current square.

To cont joining squares tog, instead of ch2 between tr, work 1dc in corresponding ch-2 sp of previous square, ch1. When next corner ch-2 sp of side has been joined, complete remaining sides as for foundation square.

Join all 12 squares.

BORDER

With RS facing, join H in any ch-2 corner sp on right-hand side at one end of scarf (opposite corner if working left-handed).

Note: When working next round, where two squares have been joined treat the joined corner as two separate ch-2 sps.

Round 1: Ch3 (counts as first tr), (2tr, ch2, 3tr) in same sp, *ch1, [3htr in next ch-2 sp, ch1] to next corner ch-2 sp of scarf, (3tr, ch2, 3tr) in corner ch-2 sp; rep from * twice more, ch1, [3htr in next ch-2 sp, ch1] to beg corner, ss in top of beg ch-3 to join.

Fasten off H.

Round 2: Join B in any corner ch-2 sp, ch2 (counts as first htr), (2htr, ch2, 3htr) in same sp, *ch1, [3htr in next ch-1 sp, ch1] to next ch-2 corner sp, (3htr, ch2, 3htr) in ch-2 corner sp; rep from * twice more, ch1, [3htr in next ch-1 sp, ch1] to beg corner, ss in top of beg ch-2 to join.

Fasten off B.

Round 3: Using F, rep round 2.

Fasten off F.

Round 4: Join D in any ch-2 corner sp, ch3 (counts as first dc and ch2), 1dc in same ch-2 sp, *1dc in each st to next corner sp, (1dc, ch2, 1dc) in ch-2 corner sp; rep from * twice more, 1dc in each st to end, ss in first of beg ch-3 to join.

Fasten off.

Making up and finishing

Sew in any ends.

Speckled Cowl

The combination of dots and stripes gets me every time and linen stitch is my all-time favourite. Here I have kept the palette down to five colours and created a striped pattern that repeats four times to bring some order to the piece. It's that black, white and grey that gives this cowl a contemporary twist.

Skill level: *

YARN AND MATERIALS

West Yorkshire Spinners The Croft Shetland Colours Aran (100% Shetland wool, approx. 166m/182yd per 100g/3½oz hank) aran (worsted) weight yarn:

1 ball each of:
Voxter shade 099 (A)
Sullom shade 010 (B)
Lerwick shade 637 (C)
Ollaberry shade 568 (D)
Melby shade 551 (E)

HOOKS AND EQUIPMENT

6mm (US size J/10) crochet hook

Yarn needle

FINISHED MEASUREMENTS

84cm (33in) long x 26cm (10¼in) wide, before joining ends

TENSION

12 sts x 11 rows measures 7cm (2¾in) square working in linen stitch patt using a 6mm (US J/10) hook, counting each ch and dc as 1 st.

ABBREVIATIONS

See page 127.

Cowl

Using C, ch46.
Row 1: 1dc in fourth ch from hook, *ch1, miss next ch, 1dc in next ch; rep from * to end changing to A on last dc, turn.
Row 2: Ch2 (counts as ch1 and 1dc), 1dc in first ch-1 sp, *ch1, 1dc in next ch-1 sp; rep from * to end changing to next colour on last dc, turn.
Rep row 2 for another 126 rows, foll colour sequence below.

Row 3:	Yarn B
Row 4:	Yarn E
Row 5:	Yarn D
Row 6:	Yarn C
Row 7:	Yarn E
Row 8:	Yarn D
Row 9:	Yarn A
Row 10:	Yarn E
Row 11:	Yarn D
Row 12:	Yarn B
Row 13:	Yarn E
Row 14:	Yarn D
Row 15:	Yarn C
Row 16:	Yarn A
Row 17:	Yarn B
Row 18:	Yarn A
Row 19:	Yarn C
Row 20:	Yarn D
Row 21:	Yarn E
Row 22:	Yarn B
Row 23:	Yarn D
Row 24:	Yarn E
Row 25:	Yarn A
Row 26:	Yarn D
Row 27:	Yarn E

See page 127.

Tips

• Always start with an even number of chain and change colour on the last yarn round hook of the current row.

• Leave 10cm (4in) yarn ends and work over them as you crochet the next row.

Row 28:	Yarn C
Row 29:	Yarn D
Row 30:	Yarn E
Row 31:	Yarn B
Row 32:	Yarn A
Row 33:	Yarn C
Row 34:	Yarn A

Rep rows 3–34 two more times, then rep rows 3–32 once.
Fasten off.

Making up and finishing

With the scarf laid out flat, take the corners of one end and flip them over to create a twist in the middle of the scarf. Using C, join the two ends together with whip stitch, preserving the twist.

Colour therapy

If you want to play with colours and see how they relate to each other, then gather your stash and have a play with linen stitch, which is the most wonderful pattern.

Twisted Headband

With so many yarns offering beautiful gradients of colour in one ball, it's lovely to combine two contrasting colour schemes into one project in the form of stripes. This popular method highlights the beauty of both palettes, as the colour patterns emerge side by side. All you need do is select two balls of yarn that have enough contrast between them to create your unique piece.

Skill level: *

YARN AND MATERIALS

Adriafil Mistero (53% wool, 47% acrylic, approx. 90m/98yd per 50g/1¾oz ball) chunky (bulky) weight yarn:
  1 ball each of:
  Danube Fancy shade 065 (A)
  Shabby Chic Fancy shade 059 (B)

HOOKS AND EQUIPMENT

6mm (US size J/10) crochet hook

Yarn needle

FINISHED MEASUREMENTS

44cm (17¼in) circumference (unstretched) x 10.5cm (4⅛in) wide

TENSION

14 sts x 12 rows measures 10.5cm (4⅛in) square working double crochet BLO using a 6mm (US size J/10) hook.

ABBREVIATIONS

See page 127.

Headband

Foundation chain: Using A, ch15.
Row 1: 1dc in second ch from hook, 1dc in each ch to end. (*14 dc*)
Row 2: Ch1 (does not count as a st throughout), 1dc BLO of each st to end, do not fasten off A.
Rows 3–4: Using B, rep row 2, do not fasten off B.
Rows 5–6: Using A, rep row 2.
Rep rows 3–6, alternating colour every two rows, until headband measures 44cm (17¼in) or desired length to fit head circumference.
Fasten off.

Making up and finishing

Using the illustration as a guide, lay the finished piece flat and fold in half lengthways just at each end. Bring both ends together as shown, so they interlock. Using A, sew through all four layers to join the ends together. Turn right side out. Voila!

Tips

• Change to the new colour on last yarn round hook on the current row.
• The number of rows can be adjusted to fit an individual head size.

I particularly love the neutral creamy mushroom greys set against the warm autumn colours – you don't need to think about colour selection too much here, just let the yarn do all the work.

chapter 4

Winter

Neon Mandalas

This is all about the neons. On their own neons are loud and capture your attention, which is why they are often used for signage and safety alerts. When combined with other neons they can lose their impact, but when set against neutral tones, they energise and enrich the greys and create quite a contemporary modern piece of crochet. The addition of silver keeps it fresh and sharp.

Skill level: **

YARN AND MATERIALS

Rico Ricorumi Neon DK (100% acrylic, 60m/65yd per 25g/⅞oz ball) DK (light worsted) weight yarn:
1 ball each of:
Orange shade 001
Fuchsia shade 002
Green shade 003

Rico Ricorumi DK (100% cotton, 57m/62yd per 25g/⅞oz ball) DK (light worsted) weight yarn:
1 ball each of:
White shade 001
Yellow shade 006
Silver Grey shade 058
Mouse Grey shade 059

Rico Ricorumi Lamé DK (62% polyester, 38% polyamide, 50m/54yd per 10g/⅓oz ball) DK (light worsted) weight yarn:
1 ball of Silver shade 001

HOOKS AND EQUIPMENT

3mm (US size C/2–D/3) crochet hook

6 metal rings, 10cm (4in) diameter

Yarn needle

FINISHED MEASUREMENTS

10cm (4in) diameter

TENSION

Rounds 1 to 3 measure 4cm (1½in) diameter working pattern using a 3mm (US size C/2–D/3) hook.

ABBREVIATIONS

See page 127.

SPECIAL ABBREVIATIONS

tr6tog (treble crochet 6 stitches together): [yarn round hook, insert hook in next stitch, yarn round hook, pull yarn through work, yarn round hook, pull yarn through first 2 loops on hook] six times (7 loops on hook), yarn round hook, pull through all loops on hook to complete cluster

edc (extended double crochet): work a double crochet stitch in the next dc two rounds below

FPdc (front post double crochet): insert hook from front to back around top of next CL, yarn round hook, draw yarn around post of stitch, yarn round hook and pull through both loops on hook

COLOUR THERAPY

These little mandalas are inspired by my inability to pass up the opportunity of working with neon pink! When I hold the pink next to the orange my heart goes into happiness overload. Notice how the neons glow with a vivid intensity when set against the whites and greys. When using neons, it's wise to follow the 'less is more' rule!

Mandala

Make a magic ring.

Round 1: Ch1 (does not count as a st), 8dc in the ring, ss in first dc to join. (*8 sts*)

Fasten off.

Round 2: Join next colour in any st, ch2 (counts as first htr), 1htr in same st, 2htr in each st to end, ss in top of beg ch-2 to join, fasten off. (*16 sts*)

Round 3: Join next colour in any st, ch1 (counts as first dc), 1dc in next st, [1edc in next st from round 1, 1dc in each of next 2 sts] 7 times, 1edc in next st from round 1, ss in beg ch-1 to join, fasten off. (*24 sts*)

Round 4: Join next colour in any st, ch1 (counts as first dc), 1dc in next st, 2dc (inc) in next st, [1dc in each of next 2 sts, 2dc (inc) in next st] 7 times, ss in beg ch-1 to join, fasten off. (*32 sts*)

Round 5: Join next colour in any inc st, ch1 (counts as first dc), ch5, [miss next 3 sts, 1dc in next inc st, ch5] 7 times, miss next 3 sts, ss in beg ch-1 to join, fasten off.

Round 6: Join next colour in any ch-5 sp, ch1 (counts as first dc), 5dc in same sp, 6dc in each ch-5 sp to end, ss in beg ch-1 to join, fasten off.

MAKE PETALS

Round 7: Join next colour in first dc of any 6-dc sequence, ch2 (counts as first st for first tr6tog), complete first tr6tog over next 5 sts (first petal made), ch8, [tr6tog, ch8] 7 times, ss in top of first tr6tog to join.

JOIN MANDALA TO HOOP

Working over metal ring and ch-8 sp throughout, place mandala inside ring with RS facing.

Round 8: Join yarn in any ch-8 sp, ch1 (counts as first dc), 7dc in same sp, 1FPdc around top of first CL, *8dc, 1FPdc around top of next CL; rep from * to end, ss in beg ch-1 to join.

Fasten off.

Making up and finishing

Sew in any ends.

Work one French knot (see page 123) in the centre of round 1, work French knots at the top of each edc from round 3 (8 French knots), and one French knot in between the third and fourth dc of every 6-dc sequence in round 6.

HANGING LOOP

Join a contrasting colour through any front post dc, ch25, ss in first ch to join.

Fasten off and sew in ends securely.

Tips

• Use any colour for any round and change colour on each round.

• When working any mandala in a hoop it's good to keep your tension tight. If your mandala is working up to be too large for the hoop, drop down a size in crochet hook.

Blue Tile Trivet

This useful trivet is inspired by all the blue willow-pattern china tea sets that I have incorporated into my mosaic work over the years. Here I have chosen to work with an array of blues across the spectrum and you can see that they all harmonise beautifully, no matter what order you place them in.

Skill level: **

YARN AND MATERIALS

Scheepjes Catona (100% cotton, approx. 63m/68yd per 25g/⅞oz ball) 4-ply (sport) weight yarn:
  1 ball each of:
  Bridal White shade 105 (A)
  Deep Amethyst shade 508 (B)
  Bluebell shade 173 (C)
  Lilac Mist shade 399 (D)
  Bluebird shade 247 (E)
  Powder Blue shade (384) (F)
  Cyan shade 397 (G)

HOOKS AND EQUIPMENT

3mm (US size C/2–D/3) crochet hook

Yarn needle

FINISHED MEASUREMENTS

22 x 22cm (8½ x 8½in)

TENSION

Rounds 1 and 2 of small tile measure 3cm (1¼in) diameter working double crochet using a 3mm (US size C/2–D/3) hook.

ABBREVIATIONS

See page 127.

SPECIAL ABBREVIATION

BPdc (back post double crochet): insert hook from back to front between posts of first and second half treble in row below and then from front to back between posts of second and third stitch, yarn round hook, draw yarn around post of stitch, yarn round hook and pull through both loops on hook

Colour combinations

When making the nine small tiles, change colour on each round but always work round 6 and either round 2 or 3 in A. This creates a gentle sense of order without it being too obvious and controlled. The use of dark blue to join and frame each tile helps create the effect of one large tile made up of nine smaller ones.

Tiles

(make 9)
Using first colour, make a magic ring.
Round 1: Ch1 (does not count as a st), 12dc into ring, ss in first dc to join, fasten off first colour.
Round 2: Join new colour in any st, ch1 (counts as 1dc), 1dc in same st, ch1, miss next st, *2dc in next st, ch1, miss next st; rep from * 4 times, ss in beg ch-1 to join, fasten off.
Round 3: Join new colour in any ch-1 sp, ch2 (counts as first htr), (1htr, ch1, 2htr) in same sp at base of ch-2, ch1, miss next 2 sts, *(2htr, ch1, 2htr) in next ch-1 sp, ch1, miss next 2 sts; rep from * 4 times, ss in top of beg ch-2 to join, fasten off.
Round 4: Join new colour in any ch-1 sp, ch2 (counts as first htr), (1htr, ch2, 2htr) in same sp (first corner made), [miss next 2 sts, 2dc in next ch-1 sp] twice, miss next 2 sts, *(2htr, ch2, 2htr) in next ch-1 sp (corner made), [miss next 2 sts, 2dc in next ch-1 sp] twice, miss next 2 sts; rep from * twice, ss in top of beg ch-2 to join, fasten off.
Round 5: Join new colour in any ch-2 corner sp, ch1 (counts as 1dc), (1dc, ch2, 2dc) in same sp for corner, [miss next 2 sts, 2dc in sp between sts] 3 times, miss next 2 sts, *(2dc, ch2, 2dc) in next ch-2 sp for corner, [miss next 2 sts, 2dc in sp between sts] 3 times, miss next 2 sts; rep from * twice, ss in beg ch-1 to join, fasten off.
Round 6: Join A in any ch-2 corner sp, ch1 (counts as 1dc), (1dc, ch2, 2dc) in same sp for corner, [miss next 2 dc, 2dc in sp between sts] 4 times, miss next 2 dc, *(2dc, ch2, 2dc) in next ch-2 sp for corner, [miss next 2 dc, 2dc in sp between sts] 4 times, miss next 2 dc; rep from * twice, ss in beg ch-1 to join.
Fasten off.

Making up and finishing

Place the nine tiles in three rows of three to make a large square, arranging them in any order that is pleasing to your eye.
JOINING TILES
Hold 2 squares with WS together and work each st through both layers.
Row 1 (RS): Join B in any ch-2 corner sp, ch1 (does not count as a st), 1dc in same ch-2 sp, 1dc in each st to next corner, 1dc in corner ch-2 sp.
Fasten off.
Rep row 1 to add a third tile to the strip.
Rep to make 3 strips of 3 tiles.
Join the 3 strips using the same method to form one large square.

BORDER
Join B in any corner ch-2 sp.
Round 1 (RS): Ch2 (counts as first htr), (1htr, ch2, 1htr) in same sp, work 40htr evenly spaced to next corner, *(2htr, ch2, 1htr) in next corner ch-2 sp, work 40htr evenly spaced to next corner; rep from * twice, ss in top of beg ch-2 to join.
Fasten off B.
Round 2: Join A in back post of any htr, ch1 (counts as first dc), *1BPdc around each htr post to corner, ch2; rep from * 3 times, 1BPdc around each htr post to end, ss in beg ch-1 to join.
Fasten off A.
Round 3: Join D in any ch-2 corner sp, ch2 (counts as first htr), (1htr, ch2, 2htr) in same sp, 1htr in each st to next corner, *(2htr, ch2, 2htr) in next ch-2 sp, 1htr in each st to next corner; rep from * twice, ss in top of beg ch-2 to join.
Fasten off D.
Round 4: Join A in any st, ch1 (counts as first dc), 1dc in each st and 3dc in each ch-2 corner sp to end, ss in beg ch-1 to join.
Fasten off.
Sew in all ends.

YARN AND MATERIALS

Rico Creative Melange Big Super Chunky (53% virgin wool, 47% acrylic, approx. 100m/109yd per 100g/3½oz ball) super chunky (super bulky) weight yarn:

Version 1:
   3 balls of Multi Grey shade 002 (A)
   1 ball of Multi Fuchsia shade 003 (B)

Version 2:
   3 balls of Grey Mouline shade 020 (A)
   1 ball Teal Turquoise shade 030 (B)

HOOKS AND EQUIPMENT

9mm (US size M/13) crochet hook

Yarn needle

40cm (16in) zip

Pins

Sewing needle and matching thread

45 x 45cm (18 x 18in) cushion pad

FINISHED MEASUREMENTS

45 x 45cm (18 x 18in)

TENSION

10 htr x 5 rows measures 15 x 11cm (6 x 4½in) working pattern (rows 2–5) using a 9mm (US size M/13) hook.

ABBREVIATIONS

See page 127.

SPECIAL ABBREVIATION

MB (make bobble): *yarn round hook, insert hook in stitch, yarn round hook, pull yarn through work, yarn round hook, pull yarn through first 2 loops on hook; rep from * 4 more times in same stitch, yarn round hook, pull through all loops on hook

Bobble Cushion

This cushion is worked in two colourways to illustrate the difference between a subtle grey background and one that has more to say with its array of black, white and grey shades. Personally I prefer the pink version, because I love the way the bobbles pop as they move against the different background tones, but the turquoise version looks lovely, too.

Tips

• Keep your work neat by working over the B colour when working the htr between bobbles.

• Change colour on the last yarn round hook of the current colour.

Cushion

(make 2, one for each side)
Work in multiples of 6 plus 1.
Foundation chain: Using A, ch31.
Row 1: 1htr in third ch from hook (missed 2 ch do not count as a st), 1htr in each ch to end. (*29 htr*)
Row 2: Ch2 (does not count as a st throughout), 1htr in each of next 2 sts, *change to B, MB, change to A, 1htr in each of next 5 sts; rep from * 3 times, change to B, MB, change to A, 1htr in each of next 2 sts, fasten off B.
Row 3: Ch2, 1htr in each st to end.
Row 4: Ch2, 1htr in each of next 5 sts, *change to B, MB, change to A, 1htr in each of next 5 sts; rep from * 2 times, change to B, MB, change to A, 1htr in each of next 5 sts, fasten off B.
Row 5: Ch2, 1htr in each st to end.
Rows 6–19: Rep rows 2–5 three times, then rep rows 2–3 once.
Fasten off.

Making up and finishing

Place the zip down right side up. Align one edge of one cushion side RS up along the zip tape so it's near the zip teeth and pin in place. Align one edge of the other cushion side along the other side of the zip teeth, making sure the bobbles on both cushion pieces run in the same direction.

Pin in place. Using a sewing needle and matching thread, sew the zip in place.
Open the zip. Fold the two sides of the cushion so they are now RS together and sew around the remaining three edges using a length of yarn. Turn the cushion RS out. Sew in any ends and then insert the cushion pad.

COLOUR THERAPY

Grey is a neutral colour and works best as a backdrop. On its own it can feel a little lifeless, but when you drop another colour onto it grey can be warm and inviting. Notice how the pink bobbles compete with their busy background to create an energised piece that has all the colours bouncing off each other. By contrast, the neutrality of the simple grey background of version 2 allows the gentle turquoise shades to present themselves without any fuss, giving a more restful feel to the cushion.

Bobble Hat

This pure wool yarn has all the squish and bounce one could dream of, making it perfect for a warm woolly hat. The pattern is inspired by beautiful Nordic knits, which are always in style.

Skill level: **

YARN AND MATERIALS

West Yorkshire Spinners The Croft Shetland Colours Aran (100% Shetland Tweed Aran, approx. 166m/182yd per 100g/3½oz hank) aran (worsted) weight yarn:

1 ball each of:
Sullom shade 010 (A)
Lerwick shade 637 (B)
Tresta shade 583 (C)
Laxfirth shade 639 (D)
Ollaberry shade 568 (E)

HOOKS AND EQUIPMENT

6mm (US size J/10) crochet hook

Yarn needle

7.5cm (3in) pompom maker

FINISHED MEASUREMENTS

52cm (20½in) circumference at widest point
48cm (19in) circumference at bottom of brim
28cm (11in) high (including pompom)

TENSION

Foundation round measures 48cm (19in) long laid flat before joining.

ABBREVIATIONS

See page 127.

SPECIAL ABBREVIATIONS

edc (extended double crochet): work a double crochet stitch in the next dc two rounds below
BPtr (back post treble): working from the back, yarn round hook, insert hook from back to front to back around post of stitch in round below, yarn round hook, draw yarn around post of stitch, [yarn round hook, pull through 2 loops] twice
FPtr (front post treble): working from the front, yarn round hook, insert hook from front to back to front around post of stitch in round below, yarn round hook, draw yarn around post of stitch, [yarn round hook, pull through 2 loops] twice
MB (make bobble): *yarn round hook, insert hook in stitch, yarn round hook, pull yarn through work, yarn round hook, pull yarn through first 2 loops on hook; rep from * 4 more times in same stitch, yarn round hook, pull yarn through all loops on hook

Hat

Worked from bottom to top.
Foundation round: Using A, ch3, yrh, insert hook in third ch from hook, yrh and pull through, ch1, [yrh, pull through 2 loops on hook] twice (first stitch complete), *yrh, insert hook in ch at base of prev st, yrh and pull through, ch1, [yrh, pull through 2 loops on hook] twice; rep from * until 60 sts have been made, ss in top of first st to join. (*60 sts*)
Rounds 2–5: Join in B in any st, *ch3 (does not count as a st), [1FPtr in next st, 1BPtr in next st] 30 times, ss in top of first FPtr to join.
Fasten off B at end of round 5.
Round 6: Join A in any st, ch2 (does not count as a st), 1htr in each st to end, ss in top of first htr to join.
Fasten off A.
Round 7: Join C in any st, ch1 (does not count as a st), 1dc in each st to end, ss in first dc to join.
Fasten off C.
Round 8: Join D in any st, ch1 (does not count as a st), 1dc in same st, *1edc in next st two rounds below, 1dc in next st; rep from * to last st, 1edc in next st two rounds below, ss in first dc to join.
Fasten off D.
Round 9: Join A in any st, rep round 7 but do not fasten off A.
Round 10: Using A, ch3 (counts as first htr), 1htr in each of next 2 sts changing to E on last yrh of second htr, MB in E changing to A on last yrh, *1htr in each of next 3 sts changing to E on last yrh of third htr, MB in E changing to A on last yrh; rep from * 13 times, using A, ss in top of beg 2-ch to join.
Fasten off E.
Round 11: Using A, rep round 7.
Fasten off A.
Round 12: Using C, rep round 7.
Fasten off C.
Round 13: Using D, rep round 8.
Round 14: Using B, rep round 6.
Round 15: Using A, rep round 6.
Round 16 (dec): Join D in any st, ch2 (does not count as a st), 1htr in same st, 1htr in each of next 7 sts, htr2tog, *1htr in each of next 8 sts, htr2tog; rep from * to end, ss in top of first htr to join. (*54 sts*)
Fasten off D.
Round 17 (dec): Join C in any st, ch2 (does not count as a st), 1htr in same st, 1htr in each of next 6 sts, htr2tog, *1htr in each of next 7 sts, htr2tog; rep from * to end, ss in top of first htr to join. (*48 sts*)
Round 18: Using A, rep round 7.
Fasten off A.

Round 19: Using E, rep round 8.
Fasten off E.

Round 20 (dec): Join A in any st, ch2 (does not count as a st), 1htr in same st, 1htr in each of next 5 sts, htr2tog, *1htr in each of next 6 sts, htr2tog; rep from * to end, ss in top of first htr to join. (*42 sts*)

Round 21 (dec): Join C in any st, ch1 (does not count as a st), 1dc in same st, 1dc in each of next 4 sts, dc2tog, *1dc in each of next 5 sts, dc2tog; rep from * to end, ss in top of first htr to join. (*36 sts*)

Round 22 (dec): Join A in any st, ch2 (does not count as a st), 1htr in same st, 1htr in each of next 3 sts, htr2tog, *1htr in each of next 4 sts, htr2tog; rep from * to end, ss in top of first htr to join. (*30 sts*)
Fasten off A.

Round 23 (dec): Join B in any st, ch2 (does not count as a st), 1htr in same st, 1htr in each of next 2 sts, htr2tog, *1htr in each of next 3 sts, htr2tog; rep from * to end, ss in top of first htr to join. (*24 sts*)

Round 24 (dec): Ch2 (does not count as a st), 1htr in same st, 1htr in next st, htr2tog, *1htr in each of next 2 sts, htr2tog; rep from * to end, ss in top of first htr to join. (*18 sts*)

Round 25 (dec): Ch2 (does not count as a st), 1htr in same st, htr2tog, *1htr in next st, htr2tog; rep from * to end, ss in top of first htr to join. (*12 sts*)

Round 26 (dec): Ch2 (does not count as a st), 1htr in same st, [htr2tog] to last st, 1htr in last st, ss in top of first htr to join. (*7 sts*)
Fasten off, weaving end through rem sts to close.

Making up and finishing

Sew in any ends.
Using all yarns, make a pompom and sew onto the top of the hat.

Rope Baskets

The combination of neutral greys and soft creamy white gives these functional baskets a very modern feel. The stitches are worked around rope to give the baskets added stability, while the white surface crochet on the inside of the large basket also helps it to keep its shape. Notice how beautifully the grey tones frame the evenly-spaced French knots, adding subtle pops of colour to the sides of the tall basket.

Skill level: **

YARN AND MATERIALS

Rico Ricorumi DK (100% cotton, approx. 57m/62yd per 25g/⅞oz ball) DK (light worsted) weight yarn:

1 ball each of:
Cream shade 002 (A)
Silver Grey shade 058 (B)
Mouse Grey shade 059 (C)
Rose shade 008 (D)
Candy Pink shade 012 (E)
Pastel Yellow shade 062 (F)

Rico Ricorumi Lamé DK (62% polyester, 38% polyamide, approx. 50m/54yd per 10g/⅓oz ball) DK (light worsted) weight yarn:
1 ball of Silver shade 001 (G)

5m (5½yd) of sisal 6mm natural rope in light brown

HOOKS AND EQUIPMENT

3.5mm (US size E/4) crochet hook

Stitch marker

Yarn needle

FINISHED MEASUREMENTS

Small basket measures 9cm (3½in) tall x 11cm (4¼in) diameter

Large basket measures 7cm (2¾in) tall x 20cm (8in) diameter

TENSION

Rounds 1–2 measure approx. 4cm (1⅝in) in diameter (worked over rope).

ABBREVIATIONS

See page 127.

SPECIAL ABBREVIATION

edc (extended double crochet): work a double crochet stitch in the next dc two rounds below

Small basket

Work with two strands of yarn held together. Change colour on last yarn round hook of current colour.
Using two strands of A held tog, make a magic ring.
Round 1: Ch1 (does not count as a st), 8dc into ring. (*8 sts*)
Work in a continuous spiral. PM in last st and move up as each round is finished.
Hold rope over top of dc in prev round and work each st as normal, working over rope throughout.
Round 2: [2dc in next st] 8 times. (*16 sts*)
Round 3: [1dc in next st, 2dc in next st] 8 times. (*24 sts*)
Round 4: [1dc in each of next 2 sts, 2dc in next st] 8 times. (*32 sts*)
Round 5: [1dc in each of next 3 sts, 2dc in next st] 8 times. (*40 sts*)
Round 6: 1dc in each of next 4 sts, 2dc in next st] 8 times. (*48 sts*)
Round 7: 1dc BLO in each st to end.
Fasten off A. Join B and C.
Cont working in a continuous spiral, moving marker up as each round is finished throughout.
Round 8: Holding B and C tog, *1dc in next st, 1edc in BLO of next st two rounds below; rep from * to end.
Round 9: 1dc in each st to end.
Fasten off B and C. Join two strands of A.
Round 10: *1dc in next st, 1edc in next st two rounds below (working through both loops); rep from * to end.
Round 11: Rep round 9.
Round 12 and 13: Using B and C held tog, rep rounds 10 and 11.
Round 14: Using two strands of A held tog, rep round 10. Cut rope.
Round 15: 1dc in each of next two sts, ss in each of next 2 sts (to smooth transition from where rope has ended).
BORDER
With RS still facing, working from left to right, ch2, work backward (crab stitch) working 1dc in each st around, ss in top of beg ch-2 to join.
Fasten off.

Large basket

Work with one strand of A and one strand of B or C held tog throughout, changing between B and C frequently as and when desired.

Rounds 1–6: Work as for small basket. (*48 sts*)

Round 7: [1dc in each of next 5 sts, 2dc in next st] 8 times. (*56 sts*)

Round 8: [1dc in each of next 6 sts, 2dc in next st] 8 times. (*64 sts*)

Round 9: [1dc in each of next 7 sts, 2dc in next st] 8 times. (*72 sts*)

Round 10: 1dc FLO in each st to end.
Working FLO turns sides inward, keeping RS facing on inside of basket.
Cont working in a continuous spiral, moving marker up as each round is finished throughout.

Rounds 11–14: 1dc in each st to end.
Cut rope.

Round 15: 1dc in each of next two sts, ss in each of next 2 sts (to smooth transition from where rope has ended).

BORDER
Using two strands of A held tog, with RS still facing, working from left to right, ch2, work backward (crab stitch) working 1dc in each st around, ss in top of beg ch-2 to join.
Fasten off.

Tips

• Gently pull the rope every 20 stitches or so to keep it tight and even.

• Sisal rope can be a little rough on the hands, so you could opt for the softer cotton cord that is often used for macramé instead.

Making up and finishing

On the small basket, work French knots (see page 123) at the base of each spike created by the edc, combining G with E for the bottom row, G and D for the middle row and G and F for the top row.

On large basket, join A at base of border round and work surface crochet around.
Fasten off.
Starting at centre of basket, along top of round 1, work surface crochet (see page 126) in A, creating a spiral ending at round 10.

Sew in ends.

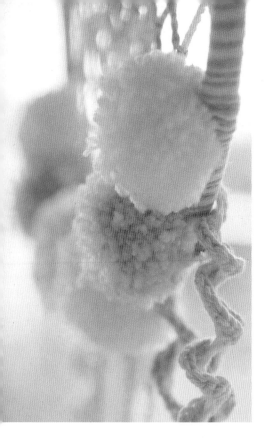

Dreamcatcher

Pretty pastels work beautifully with bright white to give a crisp, clean finish. The soft pastel pinks gently warm the cooler blues, and their unassuming neutral tones create a soothing effect. The calming nature of pastels make this dreamcatcher a great choice for a young child's room.

Skill level: **

YARN AND MATERIALS

Rico Ricorumi DK (100% cotton, approx. 57m/62yd per 25g/⅞oz ball) DK (light worsted) weight yarn:
1 ball each of:
White shade 001 (A)
Light Blue shade 033 (B)
Pink shade 011 (C)
Pastel Green shade 045 (D)
Vanilla shade 005 (E)

Stylecraft Special DK (100% acrylic, approx. 295m/322yd per 100g/3½oz ball) DK (light worsted) weight yarn:
1 ball each of:
White shade 1001 (F)
Spring Green shade 1316 (G)
Candyfloss shade 1130 (H)
Sherbet shade 1034 (I)

Approx. 100 glass beads, 4.5mm size

HOOKS AND EQUIPMENT

2.5mm (US size B/1) crochet hook

0.6mm (US size 14 steel) crochet hook

22cm (8½in) embroidery hoop, inner ring only

5cm (2in) pompom maker

Yarn needle

FINISHED MEASUREMENTS

73cm (28¾in) long (including hanging loop) x 24cm (9½in) wide

TENSION

Rounds 1–3 measure 5.5cm (2⅛in) diameter using a 2.5mm (US size B/1) hook.

ABBREVIATIONS

See page 127.

SPECIAL ABBREVIATIONS

PB dc (place bead on double crochet): insert hook in stitch, yarn round hook, pull yarn through (2 loops on hook), yarn round hook, pull through both loops to complete double crochet, remove 2.5mm (US size B/1) hook from loop, thread one bead onto 0.6mm (US size 14 steel) hook, pick up loop with 0.6mm (US size 14 steel) hook and pull through bead, remove 0.6mm (US size 14 steel) hook and pick up loop again with 2.5mm (US size B/1) hook

PB tr (place bead on treble): yarn round hook, insert hook in stitch, yarn round hook, pull yarn through work (3 loops on hook), remove 2.5mm (US size B/1) hook from third loop, thread one bead onto 0.6mm (US size 14 steel) hook, pick up loop with 0.6mm (US size 14 steel) hook and pull through bead, remove 0.6mm (US size 14 steel) hook and pick up loop again with 2.5mm (US size B/1) hook, yarn round hook, pull through first 2 loops on hook (2 loops on hook), yarn round hook, pull through both loops to complete the treble

beaded tr3tog (beaded treble 3 stitches together): [yarn round hook, insert hook in next stitch, yarn round hook, pull yarn through work, yarn round hook, pull yarn through first 2 loops on hook] 3 times (4 loops on hook), yarn round hook, pull through all loops on hook, remove 2.5mm (US size B/1) hook from loop and place one bead onto 0.6mm (US size 14 steel) hook, pick up loop with 0.6mm (US size 14 steel) hook and thread bead over loop, remove 0.6mm (US size 14 steel) hook and pick up loop again with 2.5mm (US size B/1) hook

Frame

Using 2.5mm (US size B/1) hook and holding A and C tog throughout, join around wooden hoop with a ss, 126dc around hoop, ss in first dc to join.
Fasten off C.

Mandala

Using 2.5mm (US size B/1) hook and A, make a magic ring.

Round 1: Ch3 (counts as first tr throughout), 13tr in ring, ss in top of beg ch-3 to join. (*14 sts*)
Fasten off A.

Round 2: Join B in any st, ch1, thread bead onto ch, ch7 (counts as first tr and ch4), miss next st, *PB tr in next st, ch4, miss next st; rep from * to end, ss in third ch of beg ch-7 to join. (*7 sts + 7 ch-4 sps*)
Fasten off B.

Round 3: Join C in any ch-4 sp, ch2 (counts as first htr), 5htr in same ch-4 sp, 6htr in next and each ch-4 sp to end, ss in top of beg ch-2 to join. (*42 sts*)
Fasten off C.

Round 4: Join A in first htr of any 6-htr group, ch2 (counts as first incomplete tr for tr3tog), [yarn round hook, insert hook in next stitch, yarn round hook, pull yarn through work, yarn round hook, pull yarn through first 2 loops on hook] twice, yarn round hook, pull through all loops on hook, remove 2.5mm (US size B/1) hook from loop and place one bead onto 0.6mm (US size 14 steel) hook, pick up loop with 0.6mm (US size 14 steel) hook and thread bead over loop, remove 0.6mm (US size 14 steel) hook and pick up loop again with 2.5mm (US size B/1) hook, ch4, *beaded tr3tog, ch4; rep from * to end, ss in top of first tr3tog to join.
Fasten off A.

Round 5: Join E in any ch-4 sp, *ch5, 1dc in next ch-4 sp; rep from * to end, ss in first ch of beg ch-5.
Fasten off E.

Round 6: Join D in any ch-5 sp, *ch6, 1dc in next ch-5 sp; rep from * to end, ss in first ch of beg ch-6.
Fasten off D.

Round 7: Join C in any ch-6 sp, ch1 (counts as first dc), thread bead onto ch, [ch7, PB dc in next ch-6 sp] 13 times, ch7, ss in first ch to join.
Fasten off C.

Round 8: Join B in any ch-7 sp, *ch8, 1dc in next ch-7 sp; rep from * to end, ss in first ch of beg ch-8.
Fasten off B.

Round 9: Join A in any ch-8 sp, ch1, thread bead onto ch, ch5, holding mandala inside hoop, 1dc in any st on hoop, [ch5, PB dc in next ch-8 sp, ch5, miss next 8 sts on hoop, 1dc in ninth st on hoop] 13 times, ch5, ss in first ch to join. Fasten off.

Small spirals

(make 6 in total, working row 1 with the following colour: 2 with E, 1 with B, 2 with C, 1 with D)
Using 2.5mm (US size B/1) hook and A, ch60.
Row 1: Join next colour, 2dc in second ch from hook, 2dc in each ch to end.
Fasten off.

Large spiral

Using 2.5mm (US size B/1) hook and D, ch80.
Join A, 2htr in third ch from hook, 2htr in each ch to end.
Fasten off.

Beaded chain

(make 6 in any colour)
Thread 8 beads onto yarn.
Using 2.5mm (US size B/1) hook, ch1, slide bead next to hook, *ch10, slide bead next to hook; rep from * until all beads are used.
Fasten off.

Making up and finishing

Add a tassel (see page 125) made from three strands of any colour to the bottom of each spiral and chain. Attach the large spiral to the middle of the hoop at the bottom, then add three beaded chains on each side followed by three small spirals on either side. Trim the tassels as required to create an even fringe.

Make seven pompoms – four in F, one each in G, H and I. Attach the pompoms to the frame around the bottom, using the photograph as a guide.
HANGING CHAIN
Using 2.5mm (US size B/1) hook and holding A and C tog, ch30 leaving a 20cm (8in) tail at either end.
Fasten off.
Tie each tail end to the hoop directly opposite the large spiral.

Snowdrift Throw

This lacy throw, with its rounds of muted pastel tones surrounded by a sea of white, is inspired by icy winter landscapes. With the occasional use of black adding little drops of drama, there is a sophistication in its simplicity. To create this minimalist pattern, work one motif using black in one of the rounds, and surround this motif with six others all worked in any of the cool pastel shades.

Skill level: **

YARN AND MATERIALS

Rico Creative Cotton Aran (100% cotton, approx. 85m/93yd per 50g/1¾oz ball) aran (worsted) weight yarn:

    5 balls each of Natural shade 60 (A)
    1 ball each of:
    Black shade 90 (B)
    Pastel Pink shade 02 (C)
    Light Yellow shade 63 (D)
    Vanilla shade 62 (E)
    Smokey Blue shade 31 (F)
    Ice Blue shade 33 (G)
    Aquamarine shade 42 (H)
    Powder shade 61 (I)
    Clay shade 51 (J)
    Pearl Grey shade 52 (K)
    Mouse Grey shade 28 (L)
    Silver Grey shade 22 (M)

HOOKS AND EQUIPMENT

4.5mm (US size 7) crochet hook

Yarn needle

FINISHED MEASUREMENTS

87 x 132cm (34¼ x 52in)

TENSION

Rounds 1–3 measure 8cm (3⅛in) diameter using a 4.5mm (US size 7) hook.

ABBREVIATIONS

See page 127.

COLOUR COMBINATIONS

Refer to diagram on page 85 when arranging mandalas for joining, with each Mandala 1 surrounded by alternating Mandalas 2 and 3.

MANDALA 1
Make 21 with B in any one round

MANDALA 2
Make 17 with A for round 1

MANDALA 3
Make 21 with any colour except A or B for round 1

Mandala 1

(make 21, using B in any one round)
Using first colour, make a magic ring.
Round 1: Ch3 (counts as first tr), 11tr in ring, ss in top of beg ch-3 to join. (12 tr)
Fasten off first colour.
Round 2: Join second colour in any st, ch4 (counts as first tr and ch1), [1tr in next st, ch1] 11 times, ss in third ch of beg ch-4 to join. (12 tr + 12 ch-1 sps)
Fasten off second colour.
Round 3: Join third colour in any ch-1 sp, ch3 (counts as first tr), 2tr in same ch-1 sp, [3tr in next ch-1 sp] 11 times, ss in top of beg ch-3 to join. (36 tr)
Fasten off.
Round 4: Join A in any sp (not st) between 3-tr groups, [ch6, ss in next sp between next 3-tr groups] 11 times, ch3, 1dtr in first sp to complete round.
Round 5: [Ch7, ss in next ch-6 sp] 12 times.
Fasten off.

MANDALA LAYOUT

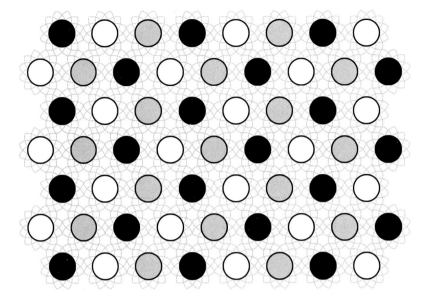

- ● Mandala 1
- ● Mandala 2
- ○ Mandala 3

Mandala 2

(make 17, using A for round 1)
Work as for Mandala 1 to end of round 3.
Fasten off.

Mandala 3

(make 21, using any colour except A or B for round 1)
Work as for Mandala 1 to end of round 3.
Fasten off.

JOIN MANDALAS
Beginning with any Mandala 2 or 3 ('current mandala'),
join A in any sp between 3-tr groups and complete
round 4 as for Mandala 1.
Each mandala is joined to its neighbour across two
corresponding ch-7 sps on round 5. Referring to diagram
on opposite page for arrangement, work round 5 on
current mandala as for Mandala 1 and at the same time
join as you go to neighbouring mandalas by replacing the
(ch-7, ss in next ch-6 sp) of round 5 with (ch3, 1dc in
corresponding ch-7 sp of neighbouring mandala, ch3,
ss in next ch-6 sp of current mandala).

Making up and finishing

Sew in all ends.
BORDER
Join A in any ch-7 sp, ch1 (counts as 1dc), 6dc in same
ch-7 sp, 7dc in each ch-7 sp and 3dc in each ch-3 sp to
end, ss in beg ch-1 to join.

COLOUR THERAPY

Incorporating tones of grey
helps to keep this piece cool,
whilst the soft pink and pale
yellow give it an unassuming
subtle lift.

chapter 5

Four Seasons

Vase of Flowers

Inspired by the rich hues and contrasting centres of anemones (my all-time favourite flowers!), this has to be one of my happiest pieces because of the colours and the fact that it's crochet flowers in all their glory. The wonderful thing is that it's relatively simple to make and you can go wild with the colours. The background is worked in two stripes of blue to add contrast and depth and by keeping the vase white, with the polka dot knots creating a symmetrical pattern, it presents the bouquet of roses and primroses in all of its colourful beauty.

Skill level: ***

YARN AND MATERIALS

Scheepjes Catona (100% cotton, approx. 63m/68yd per 25g/⅞oz ball) 4-ply (sport) weight yarn:
  1 ball each of:
  Bridal White shade 105 (A)
  Capri Blue shade 261 (B)
  Deep Amethyst shade 508 (C)

Scheepjes Catona 10g (100% cotton, approx. 25m/27yd per 10g/⅓oz ball) 4-ply (sport) weight yarn:
  1 ball each of:
  Jet Black shade 110 (D)
  Shocking Pink shade 114 (E)
  Icy Pink shade 246 (F)
  Lemon shade 280 (G)
  Tangerine shade 281 (H)
  Light Orchid shade 226 (I)
  Delphinium shade 113 (J)
  Crystalline shade 385 (K)
  Lime Juice shade 392 (L)
  Apple Granny shade 513 (M)

Rico Creative Lamé DK (62% polyester, 28% polyamide, 130m/142yd per 25g/⅞oz ball) DK (light worsted) weight yarn:
  1 ball of Gold shade 002 (N)

HOOKS AND EQUIPMENT

3mm (US size C/2–D/3) crochet hook

Yarn needle

25 x 25cm (10 x 10in) IKEA picture frame

Hot glue gun and glue sticks

FINISHED MEASUREMENTS

To fit Ikea frame 25 x 25cm (10 x 10in)
Final measurement approx. 28 x 28cm (11 x 11in) including flowers overhanging frame

TENSION

15 sts x 10 rows measures 7cm (2¾in) square working half treble using a 3mm (US size C/2–D/3) hook.

ABBREVIATIONS

See page 127.

Tips

• Quantities to make are approximate as you are encouraged to make a selection of each flower and lay them out in your own creative way to make your own unique bouquet.

• Add a single gold French knot into the centre of the flowers to give your piece added sparkle.

Vase

Foundation chain: Using A, ch6.
Row 1: 1dc in second ch from hook, 1dc in each ch to end. (*5 dc*)
Row 2: Ch1 (does not count as a st throughout), 1dc in each st to end.
Row 3: Ch1, 2dc in next st, 1dc in each of next 3 sts, 2dc in next st. (*7 dc*)
Row 4: Ch1, 1dc in each st to end.
Row 5: Rep row 3. (*9 dc*)
Row 6: Rep row 4.
Row 7: Rep row 3. (*11 dc*)
Rows 8–14: Rep row 4.
Row 15: Ch1, dc2tog, 1dc in each st to last 2 sts, dc2tog. (*9 dc*)
Row 16: Rep row 15. (*7 dc*)
Row 17: Rep row 15. (*5 dc*)
Fasten off.

Background

To fit inside mount frame (increase number of foundation ch if necessary)
Foundation chain: Using B, ch27.
Row 1: 1dc in second ch from hook, 1dc in each ch to end. (*26 dc*)

Row 2: Ch1 (does not count as a st), 1dc in each st to end.
Rows 3–32: Rep row 2, changing between B and C every 4 rows to create stripes.
Fasten off.

Note: All the roses use two colours – one for the main body and an alternative for the two central petals.

Roses

(make 14)
Combine any two colours except A, D, M or N.
Using outer colour and leaving a tail of 25cm (10in), ch21.
Row 1: 1dc in second ch from hook, 1dc in each ch to end, turn. (*20 dc*)
Row 2: Ch3 (counts as first tr), 4tr in same st at base of ch-3, ss in next st (makes first petal), [5tr in next st, ss in next st] 7 times (8 main petals made in total), change to inner colour, [5dc in next st, ss in next st] twice (two central petals made). (*10 petals*)
Fasten off – you will notice your work is curled up. This is normal!

Tiny rose bud

(make 2)
Row 1: Using outer colour, ch9, 1dc in second ch from hook, 1dc in each ch to end, turn. (*8 dc*)
Row 2: Ch3 (counts as first tr), 4tr in same st, ss in next st, [5tr in next st, ss in next st] twice, change to inner colour, 5dc in next st, ss in last st. (*4 petals*)
Fasten off leaving a 20cm (8in) tail.

Rose bud

(make 2)
Row 1: Using outer colour, ch11, 1dc in second ch from hook, 1dc in each ch to end. (*10 dc*)
Row 2: Ch3 (counts as first tr), 4tr in same st, ss in next st, [5tr in next st, ss in next st] twice, change to inner colour, [5dc in next st, ss in next st] twice. (*5 petals*)
Fasten off leaving a 20cm (8in) tail.

Primroses

(make 8)

Using any colour from E to K, or A, make a magic ring.

Round 1: Ch1 (does not count as a st), 5dc in ring, ss in first dc to join, fasten off. *(5 dc)*

Round 2: Join new colour in any st, (2tr, ss) in same st as join, *(ss, 2tr, ss) in next st; rep from * 3 times.

Fasten off.

Tiny leaf

(make approx. 4)

Using L or M, ch7, ss in second ch from hook, 1dc in next ch, 1tr in next ch, 1dtr in next ch, 1tr in next ch, 1dc in last ch.

Fasten off.

Leaf

(make approx. 9)

Using L or M, ch9, ss in second ch from hook, 1dc in next ch, 1tr in next ch, 1dtr in each of next 3 ch, 1tr in next ch, 1dc in last ch.

Fasten off.

Gold spirals

(make 2)

Using N, ch10, 3dc in second ch from hook, 3dc in each ch to end.

Fasten off.

Gold disk

Using N, make a magic ring.

Ch1 (does not count as a st), 5dc in ring, ss in first dc to join.

Fasten off.

Making up and finishing

To make up the roses, thread the needle with the tail and, beginning with the central petals, gently wrap your work around the centre to create your rose. Sew into place at the back of your rose, ensuring you sew through all layers – otherwise the centre may pop out! Using yarn N (or any colour), make a French knot (see page 123) in centre of some of the roses.

Curl up all the rose buds with the dc sts in the centre and sew together.

Fasten off.

Make a French knot in centre of round 1 of each primrose. I've used N but you can use any colour.

Using D, make series of evenly spaced French knots on the vase. Sew the vase to the background.

Place the window mount over the top of the background and arrange some of the flowers and petals to create a bouquet. Sew into place ensuring they all fit within the window mount. Once you are happy with your arrangement, glue the background onto the backing board in the frame and add the window mount on top. Add the gold disk and a few more leaves and flowers that will overlap onto the window mount. Assemble the picture frame.

Arrange clusters of remaining flowers and leaves onto each corner of the outer frame and glue into place.

Moroccan Floor Cushion

Inspired by handmade Moroccan Boucherouite rag rugs, this project uses the familiar corner-to-corner (C2C) crochet technique for the triangles, while the squares use the same technique but with blocks of treble worked from the centre in rounds. I love the effect this creates, and the colour selection for each round has a significant effect on the overall pattern. This cushion plays with the rich summer hues of mustard with orange, and deep pinks with mauve, and sets these against the occasional blue or dash of green. The use of white pushes the colours forward, but this piece could look equally as good if the white were replaced by a rich purple... imagine if you will!

Skill level: **

YARN AND MATERIALS

Paintbox Yarns Simply Chunky (100% acrylic, approx. 136m/149yd per 100g/3½oz ball) chunky (bulky) weight yarn:

    2 balls of Champagne White shade 302 (A)
    1 ball each of:
    Blood Orange shade 319
    Mustard Yellow shade 323
    Buttercup Yellow shade 322
    Spearmint Green shade 325
    Lipstick Pink shade 351
    Bubblegum Pink shade 350
    Seafoam Blue shade 331
    Raspberry Pink shade 343
    Pansy Purple shade 347
    Tea Rose shade 342

HOOKS AND EQUIPMENT

6mm (US size J/10) crochet hook

Yarn needle

Needle and thread

65 x 65cm (26 x 26in) cushion with removable plain fabric cover

FINISHED MEASUREMENTS

To fit IKEA cushion 65 x 65cm (26 x 26in)

TENSION

One smaller square (rounds 1–4) measures 14cm (5½in) square using a 6mm (US size J/10) hook.

ABBREVIATIONS

See page 127.

NOTE

'Uphill' and 'downhill' refer to different stitch sequences that are repeated for later blocks. With a downhill block you are working 3 trebles down into the side of a block from the previous round; with an uphill block you begin with ch3 and work the 3 trebles up from the side of a block from the previous round. This will become clear as you work after round 3.

Cushion

(make 4 squares with rounds 1–4, make 9 squares with rounds 1–5)

Foundation block (counts as round 1): Ch7, 1tr in fourth ch from hook, 1tr in each of next 3 ch. (*5 posts*)

Round 2:

Block 2: *Ch3, 3tr around post of last tr worked in foundation block, ch3, ss in same sp as 3-tr to complete block. (*5 posts*)

Block 3: Ch6, 1tr in fourth ch from hook, 1tr in each of next 2 ch, ss in ch-3 post sp of prev round to join. (*4 posts*)

Block 4: *Ch3, 3tr in ch-3 post sp, ch3, ss in same sp as 3-tr to complete block. (*5 posts*)

Block 5: Rep block 3. Fasten off.

Round 3:

Round 3 forms the basic pattern, with uphill and downhill sequences being worked twice for each round.

Block 6: Join new colour in ch-3 post sp of last block (block 5), rep block 4. (*5 posts*)

BEGIN DOWNHILL SEQUENCE

Block 7: 3tr in ch-3 sp of next 'step down' block (block 2), ch3, ss in same sp to complete block. (*4 posts*)

Block 8: Rep block 3. (*4 posts*)

BEGIN UPHILL SEQUENCE

Block 9: Working into same ch-3 post sp as last ss of prev block, ch3, 3tr in same sp at base of ch-3, ss in adjoining ch-3 sp in neighbouring block (block 3) to join. (*4 posts*)

Block 10: Rep block 4. (*5 posts*)

CORNER TO CORNER ORDER OF BLOCKS

KEY

Round 2

Round 3

Round 4

→ downhill block

→ uphill block

		Round 4 Block 20		
	Round 4 Block 21	Round 3 Block 8	Round 4 Block 19	
Round 4 Block 22	Round 3 Block 9	Round 2 Block 2	Round 3 Block 7	Round 4 Block 18
Round 4 Block 23	Round 3 Block 10	Round 2 Block 3	Round 1 Foundation block	Round 2 Block 5	Round 3 Block 6	Round 4 Block 17
Round 4 Block 24	Round 3 Block 11	Round 2 Block 4	Round 3 Block 13	Round 4 Block 16
	Round 4 Block 25	Round 3 Block 12	Round 4 Block 15	
		Round 4 Block 14		

BEGIN DOWNHILL SEQUENCE
Block 11: Rep block 7. (*4 posts*)
Block 12: Rep block 3. (*5 posts*)

BEGIN UPHILL SEQUENCE
Block 13: Rep block 9.
Fasten off.
Round 4: Join new colour in ch-3 sp of block 12, rep round 3, working blocks 7, 9, 11 and 13 twice.
(*25 blocks worked in total*)
Round 5: Join A in ch-3 sp of block 23, rep round 4, working blocks 7, 9, 11 and 13 three times.
Fasten off.

Side triangle

(make 8)
Work in rows from right to left with RS facing throughout.
Foundation block (counts as row 1): Ch7, 1tr in fourth ch from hook, 1tr in each of next 3 ch. (*5 posts*)
Row 2:
Block 2: Ch3, 3tr around post of last tr worked in foundation block, ch3, ss in same sp as 3-tr to join. (*5 posts*)
Block 3: Ch6, 1tr in fourth ch from hook, 1tr in each of next 2 ch, ss in ch-3 post sp of prev row to join. (*4 posts*)
Block 4: *Ch3, 3tr in ch-3 post sp, ch3, ss in same sp as 3-tr to complete block. (*5 posts*)
Fasten off.

Row 3:
Block 5: Join new colour in first ch-3 sp on block 2, ch6, 1tr in fourth ch from hook, 1tr in each of next 2 ch, ss in last ch-3 post sp of block 2 to join.

BEGIN UPHILL SEQUENCE
Block 6: Working in same ch-3 sp as last ss of prev block, ch3, 3tr in same sp, ss in adjoining ch-3 sp in neighbouring block 3 to join. (*4 posts*)
Block 7: Ch3, 3tr in same sp, ch3, ss in same sp to complete block.

COLOUR THERAPY

Arrange your yarn in colour pairings so that you have the oranges with the yellows, the pinks with the lilacs, and the blues with the greens, and use these as your starting point for some of your squares. Notice the effect the central colour has on the pairings and play with the many combinations available. By using brighter or darker colours for the centre, they sit in contrast to the surrounding colours, thus creating a square within a square.

BEGIN DOWNHILL SEQUENCE

Block 8: 3tr in ch-3 sp of next 'step down' block (block 4), ch3, ss in same sp to complete block. (*4 posts*)

Block 9: Ch6, 1tr in fourth ch from hook, 1tr in each of next 2 ch, ss in last ch-3 sp of block 4 to join.
Fasten off.

Row 4:

Block 10: Join new colour in ch-3 sp of block 5, *ch3, 3tr in same sp, ch3, ss in same sp to complete block. (*5 posts*)

Blocks 11–13: Follow downhill patt, working block 8 twice.

Block 14–16: Follow uphill patt, working block 6 twice.
Fasten off.

Corner 'half' triangle

(make 4)

Work in rows from right to left with RS facing throughout.

Foundation block (counts as row 1): Ch7, 1tr in fourth ch from hook, 1 tr in each of next 3 ch. (*5 posts*)

Row 2:

Block 2: Ch3, 3tr around post of last tr worked in foundation block, ch3, ss in same sp as 3-tr to join. (*5 posts*)

Block 3: Ch6, 1tr in fourth ch from hook, 1tr in each of next 2 ch, ss in ch-3 post sp of prev row to join. (*4 posts*)

Row 3:

Block 4: Join new colour in first ch-3 sp of block 2, ch6, 1tr in fourth ch from hook, 1tr in each of next 2 ch, ss in last ch-3 post sp of block 2 to join.

BEGIN UPHILL SEQUENCE

Block 5: Working in same ch-3 sp of block 2, ch3, 3tr in same sp, ch3, ss in adjoining ch-3 sp of block 3 to complete block. (*4 posts*)

Block 6: Ch3, 3tr in same ch-3 sp of block 3, ch3, ss in same sp to complete block.

Row 4:

Block 7: Join new colour in ch-3 sp of block 4, *ch3, 3tr in same sp, ch3, ss in same sp to complete block. (*5 posts*)

BEGIN DOWNHILL SEQUENCE

Blocks 8–9: 3tr in ch-3 sp of next 'step down' block, ch3, ss in same sp to join.

Block 10: Rep block 3.
Fasten off.

Making up and finishing

Position all the finished pieces together with WS facing to form a square and sew them together using A. Sew into the back loop stitches only so that the stitching is invisible when seen from the right side. Do not sew too tightly.

BORDER

Round 1: Join A in any ch-3 corner sp, ch6 (counts as first tr and ch-3), 1tr in same sp (first corner made), work 1tr in each st and 3tr in each ch-3 sp to next corner, *(1tr, 3ch, 1tr) in sp for corner, work 1tr in each st and 3tr in each ch-3 sp to next corner; rep from * twice, ss in 3rd ch of beg ch-6 to join.

Round 2: Ch1 (counts as first dc), (1dc, 3ch, 2dc) in ch-3 corner sp, 1dc in each st to next corner sp, *(2dc, 3ch, 2dc) in next corner sp, 1dc in each st to next corner sp; rep from * twice, ss in beg ch-1 to join.
Fasten off.

Sew in ends.

Sew the crochet piece onto the front of the cushion cover using a needle and thread.

Festival Bunting

With such rich colours, inspired by the Hindu Holi Festival, it's tempting to go wild and mix them all up, but there is a little order to this design. The black and white roundels bring it all together, giving structure while allowing the colours to do their thing.

Skill level: *

YARN AND MATERIALS

Scheepjes Cahlista Aran Cotton (100% natural cotton, 85m/93yd per 50g/1¾oz ball) Aran (worsted) weight yarn:
1 ball each of:
Bridal White shade 105 (A)
Lemon shade 280 (B)
Shocking Pink shade 114 (C)
Sweet Orange shade 411 (D)
Orange shade 189 (E)
Tulip shade 222 (F)
Lavender shade 520 (G)
Crystalline shade 385 (H)
Bluebird shade 247 (I)
Deep Amethyst shade 508 (J)
Jade shade 514 (K)
Apple Granny shade 513 (L)
Cyan shade 397 (M)
Jet Black shade 110 (N)

Rico Ricorumi Lamé DK (62% polyester, 28% polyamide, 50m/54yd per 10g/⅓oz ball) DK (light worsted) weight yarn:
1 ball of Gold shade 002 (O)

HOOKS AND EQUIPMENT

4mm (US size G/6) crochet hook

Yarn needle

FINISHED MEASUREMENTS

146cm (57½in) long x 15cm (6in) deep

TENSION

Rounds 1–4 measure 6cm (2⅜in) diameter using a 4mm (US size G/6) hook.

ABBREVIATIONS

See page 127.

SPECIAL ABBREVIATIONS

5trPC (5-treble popcorn): 5tr into space indicated, slip loop off hook, insert hook from front to back in top of first of 5-tr just made, replace loop on hook, yarn round hook and draw through both loops on hook
edc (extended double crochet): work a double crochet stitch in the next dc two rows below

Triangle

(make 7)
Using any colour, make a magic ring.
Round 1: Ch2 (counts as first htr), ch1, [1htr, ch1] 5 times into ring, ss in top of beg ch-2 to join, fasten off. (*6 htr + 6 ch-1 sps*)
Round 2: Join first colour in any ch-1 sp, *5trPC in ch-1 sp, ch6, miss next st, miss next ch-1 sp, miss next st; rep from * twice, ss in top of first PC to join, fasten off.
Round 3: Join new colour in any remaining ch-1 sp from round 1 and work over ch-6 from prev round, *5trPC in ch-1 sp, ch6, miss next st, miss next PC, miss next st; rep from * twice, ss in top of first PC to join, fasten off.
Round 4: Join A in any ch-6 sp from round 3, ch2 (counts as first htr), 8htr in same sp, *ch4, 9htr in next ch-6 sp; rep from * once, ch4, ss in top of beg ch-2 to join, fasten off.
Round 5: Join new colour in any ch-4 sp, ch3 (counts as first tr), (2tr, ch3, 3tr) in same sp (corner made), [miss next 2 sts, 3htr in next st] twice, miss next 3 sts, *(3tr, ch3, 3tr) in next ch-4 sp, [miss next 2 sts, 3htr in next st] twice, miss next 3 sts; rep from * once, ss in top of beg ch-3 to join.
Round 6: Join new colour in any ch-3 corner sp, ch3 (counts as first tr), (2tr, ch3, 3tr) in same sp (corner made), [miss next 3 sts, 3htr in sp between sts] 3 times, miss next 3 sts, *(3tr, ch3, 3tr) in next ch-3 sp, [miss next 3 sts, 3htr in sp between sts] 3 times, miss next 3 sts; rep from * once, ss in top of beg ch-3 to join.
Round 7: Join O in any ch-3 corner sp, ch1 (does not count as a st), *(2dc, ch3, 2dc) in 3-ch sp (corner made), [ch2, miss next 3 sts, 2dc in sp between sts] 4 times, ch2, miss next 3 sts; rep from * twice more, ss in first dc to join.

Round 8: Join A in any ch-3 corner sp, ch1 (does not count as a st), *(2dc, ch2, 2dc) in 3-ch sp (corner made), [ch2, miss next 2 sts, 2dc in next ch-2 sp] 5 times, ch2, miss next 2 sts; rep from * twice more, ss in first dc to join, fasten off.

Round 9: Join new colour in any ch-2 corner sp, ch1 (counts as first dc), (1dc, ch2, 2dc) in same sp (corner made), [ch2, 1edc in each of next 2 dc in O from round 7] 6 times, (2dc, ch2, 2dc) in next corner sp; rep from * once, [ch2, 1edc in each of next 2 dc in O from round 7] 6 times, ch2, ss in beg ch-1 to join.
Fasten off.

Roundel

(make 6)
Using N, make a magic ring.
Round 1: Ch1 (does not count as st), 8dc into ring, ss in first dc to join, fasten off. (*8 dc*)
Round 2: Join A in any st, ch3 (counts as first tr), 1tr in same st, 2tr in each st around, ss in top of beg ch-3 to join, fasten off. (*16 tr*)
Round 3: Join N in any st, ch1 (counts as first dc), *ch1, 1dc in next st; rep from * to end, ch1, ss in beg ch-1 to join, fasten off.
Using yarn needle, thread 2 contrasting colours together and join into back of roundel. Twist threads tog between thumb and finger to create baker's twine effect and weave through all tr posts of round 2. Use O to make a French knot (see page 123) in centre of roundel.
Sew in ends to secure.

Making up and finishing

Using O, work surface crochet (see page 126) over the top of round 1 of each triangle.
Sew in all ends.
Lay the triangles out in a line in your desired order, with a roundel between each pair.

JOIN TRIANGLES AND ROUNDELS
Row 1: With first triangle RS facing, join N in any ch-2 corner sp, ch2 (counts as 1htr), *[ch2, miss next 2 dc, 2dc in next ch-2 sp] 7 times, ch2, miss next 2 dc, 1htr in next ch-2 corner sp, ch1, join roundel by working 1tr in any ch-1 sp, ch1, miss next dc, 1tr in next ch-1 sp of roundel, ch1, 1htr in ch-2 corner space of next triangle; rep from * until all 7 triangles and 6 roundels are joined, ending with 1htr in last ch-2 corner sp of last triangle, joining A in last yarn round hook of htr.
Row 2: Using A, ch1 (does not count as a st), 1dc in first st, *[1edc in each of next 2 sts (working into round 9 of triangle), ch2, miss next 2 sts] 8 times, 2dc in ch-1 sp between 2-tr joining roundel, ch2, miss next htr from row 1; rep from * 5 times, [1edc in each of next 2 sts, ch2, miss next 2 sts] 7 times, 1edc in each of next 2 sts, 1dc in last htr, joining I on last yarn round hook of this row.
Row 3: Using I, ch1 (does not count as a st), 1dc in first st, *[ch2, miss next 2 sts, 1edc in each of next 2 sts (working into row 1)] 7 times, [ch2, miss next 2 dc, 1edc in each of next 2 sts from row 1 linking roundel] twice; rep

Tip
• Unless specified you are free to work any colour combinations you choose, but always use yarn A for rounds 4 and 7.

from * 5 times, [ch2, miss next 2 sts, 1edc in each of next 2 sts] 7 times, ch2, miss next 2 sts, 1dc in last st, joining C on last yarn round hook of this row.
Row 4: Using C, ch1 (does not count as a st), 1dc in first st, *1edc in each of next 2 sts (working into row 2), ch2, miss next 2 sts; rep from * to end, working final rep as 1edc in each of next 2 sts, 1dc in last st.
Fasten off and sew in ends.

HANGING LOOPS
Join C in first st of last row, ch20, ss in same st as join to form a loop, fasten off.
Repeat at other end and sew in any ends.

Yarn-bombed Stool

A riot of colour, with pops of neon set against black and white monochrome, makes this a feast for the eyes… although it is possible to have too much colour, the black and white brings some order to the chaos. I have outlined the colour sequence for the main granny square but have left the legs to you, dear friends! Let yourself go with the colours – just remembering to use black and white every so often.

Skill level: **

YARN AND MATERIALS

Stylecraft Special DK (100% acrylic, approx. 295m/322yd per 100g/3½oz ball) DK (light worsted) weight yarn:
  1 ball each of:
  Jaffa shade 1256 (A)
  Fiesta shade 1257 (B)
  Cream shade 1005 (C)
  Turquoise shade 1068 (D)
  Sunshine shade 1114 (E)
  Spring Green shade 1316 (F)
  Bright Green shade 1259 (G)
  Black shade 1002 (H)
  Candyfloss shade 1130 (I)
  Lavender shade 1188 (J)

Cygnet Yarns Little Ones DK (100% acrylic, approx. 66m/72yd per 25g/⅞oz ball) DK (light worsted) weight yarn:
  1 ball of High Viz Yellow shade 972 (K)

IKEA FLISAT child's stool, 24 x 24cm (9½ x 9½in), 28cm (11in) tall

HOOKS AND EQUIPMENT

3.5mm (US size E/4) crochet hook

Yarn needle

5cm (2in) pompom maker

FINISHED MEASUREMENTS

24 x 24cm (9½ x 9½in), 28cm (11in) tall

Granny square top measures 25cm (10in) square, 4cm (1½in) deep

Legs measure 11 x 25cm (4⅜ x 10in) before being sewn up

TENSION

Rounds 1 and 2 of Granny square top measure 5cm (2in) square using a 3.5mm (US size E/4) hook.

ABBREVIATIONS

See page 127.

COLOUR THERAPY

What makes this colour scheme the right side of crazy is the use of black and white. The calming influence of these neutral colours acts not only to stabilize the piece, but also as a bridge between one colour grouping and the next, so that competing colours will not be jarring.

Colour combinations

GRANNY SQUARE TOP

Round 1	Yarn A
Round 2	Yarn B
Round 3	Yarn C
Round 4	Yarn G
Round 5	Yarn D
Round 6	Yarn C
Round 7	Yarn E
Round 8	Yarn A
Round 9	Yarn C
Round 10	Yarn B
Round 11	Yarn F
Round 12	Yarn C
Round 13	Yarn K
Round 14	Yarn G
Round 15	Yarn C
Round 16	Yarn H

Granny square top

Using A, make a magic ring.
Round 1 (RS): Ch5 (counts as 1tr and ch2 throughout), [3tr, ch2] 3 times into ring, 2tr into ring, ss in third ch of beg ch-5 to join. (*Four 3-tr groups + 4 ch-2 sps*)
Fasten off A.
Round 2: Join B in any ch-2 sp, ch5 (counts as 1tr and ch2 throughout, 3tr in same sp, ch1, [(3tr, ch2, 3tr) in next ch-2 sp, ch1] 3 times, 2tr in same sp as beg ch-5, ss in third ch of beg ch-5 to join. (*Eight 3-tr groups + 4 ch-2 sps + 4 ch-1 sps*)
Fasten off B.
Round 3: Join C in any ch-2 sp, ch5, 3tr in same sp, ch1, *3tr in next ch-1 sp, ch1, (3tr, ch2, 3tr) in next ch-2 corner sp, ch1; rep from * twice more, 3tr in next ch-1 sp, ch1, 2tr in same sp as beg ch-5, ss in third ch of beg ch-5 to join. (*Twelve 3-tr groups + 4 ch-2 sps + 8 ch-1 sps*)
Fasten off C.
Round 4: Join G in any ch-2 sp, ch5, 3tr in same sp, ch1, *[3tr in next ch-1 sp, ch1] to next corner ch-2 sp, (3tr, ch2, 3tr) in ch-2 corner sp, ch1; rep from * twice more, [3tr in next ch-1 sp, ch1] to end, 2tr in same sp as beg ch-5, ss in third ch of beg ch-5 to join.
Fasten off G.
Rounds 5–10: Work as for round 4, changing colour each round. (*Forty 3-tr groups + 4 ch-2 sps + 36 ch-1 sps*)

SIDES
Rounds 11–16: Changing colour on each round, ch3 (counts as 1tr), 2tr in same sp, ch1, [3tr in next ch sp, ch1] to end, ss in top of beg ch-3 to join. (*Forty 3-tr groups + 40 ch-1 sps*)
Fasten off.

Legs

(make 4)
Change colour each row in any colour sequence you choose.
Foundation chain: Ch18.
Row 1: 1htr in third ch from hook (missed 2-ch do not count as a st), 1htr in each ch to end, change to new colour on last yrh for every new row. (*16 sts*)
Rows 2–30: Ch2 (does not count as a st throughout), 1htr in each st to end. (*16 htr*)
Fasten off.

Making up and finishing

Fold each leg over with RS tog and sew along the seam to make 4 tubes. Turn RS out and fit a tube around each leg of the stool.

Make 16 pompoms: 4 each in C and H and the remainder in your choice of colours.
Thread a wooden bead onto the tie of each pompom.
Sew pompoms along the sides of the Granny square top, spacing them evenly and positioning one C pompom and one H pompom on each corner.

Place the granny square top over the seat of the stool.

Namaste Heart

There is balance to this glorious riot of colour thanks to the defining qualities of black and white. The popcorn dots of white around the black border are a bold statement, which are reflected back in reverse with the black centres of each flower. Inspired by my love of traditional tattoo art, the wording in the banner can be worked to read whatever feels right for you.

Skill level: ***

YARN AND MATERIALS

Rico Ricorumi DK (100% cotton, approx. 57m/62yd per 25g/⅞oz ball) DK (light worsted) weight yarn:

2 balls of Fuchsia shade 014 (A)
1 ball each of:
Black shade 060 (C)
White shade 001 (D)
Purple shade 020 (F)
Wine Red shade 029 (G)
Pink shade 011 (H)
Light Green shade 046 (I)
Grass Green shade 044 (J)
Tangerine shade 026 (K)
Yellow shade 006 (L)
Sky Blue shade 031 (M)
Lilac shade 017 (N)

Rico Ricorumi Neon DK (100% acrylic, approx. 60m/65yd per 25g/⅞oz ball) DK (light worsted) weight yarn:
2 balls of Fuchsia shade 002 (B)

Rico Ricorumi Lamé DK (62% polyester, 38% polyamide, approx. 50m/54yd per 10g/⅓oz ball) DK (light worsted) weight yarn:
1 ball of Gold shade 002 (E)

HOOKS AND EQUIPMENT

4mm (US size G/6) and 3.5mm (US size E/4) crochet hooks

Yarn needle

FINISHED MEASUREMENTS

33cm (13in) wide x 34cm (13⅜in) high

TENSION

10 sts x 12 rows measures approx. 7cm (2 ¾in) square working double crochet using a 4mm (US size G/6) hook and a strand each of yarn A and B held together.

Small flower measures approx. 4.5cm (1¾in) diameter.

ABBREVIATIONS

See page 127.

SPECIAL ABBREVIATIONS

3dtrCL (3-double treble cluster):
*yarn round hook twice, insert hook in stitch, yarn round hook, pull through the work, [yarn round hook, pull through 2 loops on the hook] twice; rep from * twice more, yarn round hook, pull through all loops on hook to complete cluster

4dtrCL (4-double treble cluster):
*yarn round hook twice, insert hook in stitch, yarn round hook, pull through the work, [yarn round hook, pull through 2 loops on the hook] twice; rep from * 3 more times, yarn round hook, pull through all loops on hook to complete cluster

4trPC (4-treble popcorn): inserting hook in same stitch each time, work 4 complete trebles, slip hook out of last loop on hook and insert it into top of first stitch, then insert hook back into loop of last stitch again, yarn round hook, pull through loop on hook and first stitch to join and complete popcorn

picot (make picot): ch3, ss in third ch from hook

Heart

Using 4mm (US size G/6) hook and holding A and B tog, ch2.
Row 1: 2dc in second ch from hook, turn. (2 sts)
Row 2: Ch1 (does not count as a st throughout), 2dc in each st to end, turn. (4 sts)
Row 3 (inc): Ch1, 2dc in first st, 1dc in each st to last st, 2dc in last st, turn. (6 sts)
Row 4: Rep row 3. (8 sts)
Row 5: Ch1, 1dc in each st to end, turn.
Row 6: Rep row 3. (10 sts)
Row 7: Rep row 3. (12 sts)
Row 8: Rep row 5.
Row 9: Rep row 3. (14 sts)
Row 10: Rep row 5.
Row 11: Rep row 3. (16 sts)
Row 12: Rep row 5.
Row 13: Rep row 3. (18 sts)
Row 14: Rep row 3. (20 sts)
Row 15: Rep row 5.
Row 16: Rep row 3. (22 sts)
Row 17: Rep row 3. (24 sts)
Row 18: Rep row 3. (26 sts)
Row 19: Rep row 5.
Row 20: Rep row 3. (28 sts)
Rows 21–24: Rep row 5.
Row 25: Rep row 3. (30 sts)
Rows 26–27: Rep row 5.
Row 28: Rep row 3. (32 sts)
Row 29–30: Rep row 5.
Row 31: Rep row 3. (34 sts)
Rows 32–34: Rep row 5.

CURVES AT TOP OF HEART
Row 35: Ch1, 1dc in each of next 17 sts, turn leaving rem sts unworked. (17 sts)
Row 36: Ch1, dc2tog, 1dc in each st to end, turn. (16 sts)

Row 37: Ch1, 1dc in each st to last 2 sts, dc2tog, turn. (*15 sts*)
Row 38: Rep row 36. (*14 sts*)
Row 39: Ch1, dc2tog, 1dc in each st to last 2 sts, dc2tog, turn. (*12 sts*)
Rows 40–43: Rep row 39. (*4 sts*)
Fasten off.
Rejoin A and B in next unworked st of row 34 and cont as foll:
Row 35: Ch1, 1dc in each st to end, turn. (*17 sts*)
Row 36: Ch1, 1dc in each st to last 2 sts, dc2tog, turn. (*16 sts*)
Row 37: Ch1, dc2tog, 1dc in each st to end, turn. (*15 sts*)
Row 38: Rep row 36. (*14 sts*)
Row 39: Ch1, dc2tog, 1dc in each st to last 2 sts, dc2tog, turn. (*12 sts*)
Rows 40–43: Rep row 39. (*4 sts*)
Fasten off.

BORDER
Using 3.5mm (US size E/4) hook, rejoin A and B at bottom centre of heart.
Round 1: Ch1, 2dc in point of heart, work 57 evenly-spaced dc around edge to top centre of heart, dc2tog over top centre indent (makes central st), work 57dc around other half of heart, 2dc in point of heart, ch2, ss in top of first dc to join. (*119 sts + 1 ch-2 sp*)
Fasten off A and B.
Round 2: Join C in ch-2 sp, ch1, 2dc in same ch-2 sp, 1dc in each of next 37 sts, 2dc in next st, [1dc in each of next 2 sts, 2dc in next st] 4 times, 1dc in each of next 8 sts, dc3tog (first side complete), 1dc in each of next 8 sts, 2dc in next st, [1dc in each of next 2 sts, 2dc in next st] 4 times, 1dc in each of next 37 sts, 2dc in ch-2 sp, ch2, ss in first dc to join. (*131 sts + 1 ch-2 sp*)

Round 4: Cont with C, ch1 (does not count as a st), 1dc in each st around to first ch-1 sp, 1dc in first ch-1 sp, ch3, 1dc in second ch-1 sp, 1dc in each st to end, ss in first dc to join. *(152 sts + 1 ch-3 sp)*
Fasten off C.

Round 5: Join E in ch-3 sp, ch1 (does not count as a st), 1dc in ch-3 sp, picot, ch1, miss next st, *1dc in next st, picot, ch1, miss next st; rep from * to end, ss in first dc to join.
Fasten off.

Sash

Using 3.5mm (US size E/4) hook and D, ch3.
Row 1 (RS): 1dc in second ch from hook, 1dc in next ch, turn. *(2 sts)*
Row 2: Ch1 (does not count as a st throughout), 2dc in first st, 1dc in next st, turn. *(3 sts)*
Row 3: Ch1, 1dc in each of first 2 sts, 2dc in next st, turn. *(4 sts)*
Row 4: Ch1, 2dc in first st, 1dc in each of next 3 sts, turn. *(5 sts)*
Row 5: Ch1, 1dc in each of first 4 sts, 2htr in next st, turn. *(6 sts)*
Row 6: Ch2 (does not count as a st throughout), 2htr in first st, 1htr in next st, 1dc in each of next 4 sts, turn. *(7 sts)*
Row 7: Ch1, 1dc in each of first 4 sts, 1htr in each of next 2 sts, 2htr in last st, turn. *(8 sts)*
Row 8: Ch2, 2htr in first st, 1htr in each of next 3 sts, 1dc in each of next 4 sts, turn. *(9 sts)*
Row 9: Ch1, 1dc in each of first 4 sts, 1htr in each of next 4 sts, 2htr in last st, turn. *(10 sts)*
Row 10: Ch2, 1htr in each of first 6 sts, 1dc in each of next 4 sts, turn.
Row 11: Ch1, 1dc in each of next 4 sts, 1htr in each of next 6 sts, turn.
Rows 12–25: Rep rows 10–11 seven times.
Rows 26–41: Ch1, 1dc in each st to end, turn.
Row 42: Ch1, 1dc in each of next 4 sts, 1htr in each of next 6 sts, turn.
Row 43: Ch2, 1htr in each of next 6 sts, 1dc in each of next 4 sts, turn.
Rows 44–45: Rep rows 42–43.
Row 46: Ch1, 1dc in each of next 4 sts, 1htr in each of next 4 sts, htr2tog, turn. *(9 sts)*
Row 47: Ch2, htr2tog, 1htr in each of next 3 sts, 1dc in each of next 4 sts. *(8 sts)*
Row 48: Ch1, 1dc in each of next 4 sts, 1htr in each of next 2 sts, htr2tog, turn. *(7 sts)*
Row 49: Ch2, htr2tog, 1htr in next st, 1dc in each of next 4 sts, turn. *(6 sts)*
Row 50: Ch1, 1dc in each of next 4 sts, htr2tog, turn. *(5 sts)*
Row 51: Ch1, dc2tog, 1dc in each of next 3 sts, turn. *(4 sts)*
Row 52: Ch1, 1dc in each of next 2 sts, dc2tog, turn. *(3 sts)*
Row 53: Ch1, dc3tog.
Fasten off.

Tip

• Working the lettering can be fiddly so take your time!

POPCORN BORDER

In next round use D for popcorn sts and cont with C for other sts, changing between C and D on last yarn round hook of prev st.

Round 3: Using C, ch2 (counts as first htr), 1htr in next st, 4trPC in next st, [1htr in each of next 3 sts, 4trPC in next st] 8 times, [1htr in next st, 2htr in next st, 1htr in next st, 4trPC in next st] 7 times, 1htr in each of next 2 sts, 4trPC in central st, 1htr in each of next 2 sts, 4trPC in next st, [1htr in next st, 2htr in next st, 1htr in next st, 4trPC in next st] 7 times, [1htr in each of next 3 sts, 4trPC in next st] 8 times, 1htr in each of next 2 sts, (2htr, ch1, 4trPC, ch1, 2htr) in ch-2 sp, ss in top of beg ch-2 to join. *(150 sts + 2 ch-1 sps)*
Fasten off D.

SASH BORDER

Round 1: With RS facing, join D in any st, ch1, *work dc evenly along each edge to tip, 3dc in tip; rep from * once, work dc evenly to end, ss in first dc to join.
Fasten off.

LETTERING

Using 3.5mm (US size E/4) hook and C and F held tog, work surface crochet (see page 126) In lettering of your choice, or use the photograph on page 101 as a guide.

Sash tips

(make 2)
Using 3.5mm (US size E/4) hook and D, ch11.
Row 1: 1dc in second ch from hook, 1dc in each ch to end, turn. (*10 dc*)
Rows 2–4: Ch1 (does not count as a st throughout), 1dc in each st to end, turn.
Row 5: Ch1, 1dc in each of next 5 sts, turn. (*5 sts*)
Row 6: Ch1, dc2tog, 1dc in each of next 3 sts, turn. (*4 sts*)
Row 7: Ch1, 1dc in each of next 2 sts, dc2tog, turn. (*3 sts*)
Row 8: Ch1, dc2tog, 1dc in last st, turn. (*2 sts*)
Row 9: Ch1, dc2tog, turn. (*1 st*)
Row 10: Ch1, 1dc.
Fasten off.
Rejoin yarn in next unworked st of row 5.
Row 5: Ch1, 1dc in each of next 5 sts, turn. (*5 sts*)
Row 6: Ch1, 1dc in each of next 3 sts, dc2tog, turn. (*4 sts*)
Row 7: Ch1, dc2tog, 1dc in each of next 2 sts, turn. (*3 sts*)
Row 8: Ch1, 1dc in first st, dc2tog, turn. (*2 sts*)
Row 9: Ch1, dc2tog, turn. (*1 st*)
Row 10: Ch1, 1dc
Fasten off.

SASH TIPS BORDER

Round 1: Join D at beg of row 1, ch1 (does not count as a st), work 8 evenly-spaced dc to tip, 3dc in tip, work 5 evenly-spaced dc to 'valley', work 5 evenly-spaced dc to next tip, 3dc in second tip, work 8 evenly-spaced dc to end of row 1.
Fasten off.

Small flowers

(make 9)
Using 3.5mm (US size E/4) hook and C, make a magic ring.
Round 1: Ch2 (counts as first htr), 9htr into ring, ss in top of beg ch-2 to join. (*10 sts*)
Fasten off C.
Round 2: Join second colour in any st, *ch3, 3dtrCL in next st, ch3, ss in next st; rep from * 4 more times (5 petals made), ending final rep with a ss in base of beg ch-3 to join.
Fasten off.

Large flowers

(make 2 with petals in G, 1 with petals in H)
Using 3.5mm (US size E/4) hook and C, make a magic ring.
Round 1: Ch2 (counts as first htr), 9htr into ring, ss in top of beg ch-2 to join. (*10 sts*)
Fasten off C.
Round 2: Join second colour in any st, *ch3, 3dtrCL in next st, ch3, ss in next st; rep from * 4 more times (5 petals made), ending final rep with a ss in base of beg ch-3 to join.
Round 3: Working into back of petals, *ch2, 1dc around middle post of next 3dtrCL petal; rep from * 4 more times, ch2, ss in first ch-2 sp to join.
Round 4: (Ch3, 4dtrCL, ch3, ss) in same ch-2 sp, *(ss, ch3, 4dtrCL, ch3, ss) in next ch-2 sp; rep from * 3 more times, ss in base of beg ch-3 to join.
Fasten off.

Leaves

(make 8 in I, 15 in J)
Using 3.5mm (US size E/4) hook and I or J, ch9.
Ss in second ch from hook, 1dc in next ch, 1tr in next ch, 1dtr in each of next 3 ch, 1tr in next ch, 1dc in last ch.
Fasten off.

Polka dots

(make 5 in any colour)
Using any colour, make a magic ring.
Ch1 (does not count as a st), 8dc in ring, ss in first dc to join.
Fasten off.

Making up and finishing

Sew in any ends.

Using 3.5mm (US size E/4) hook and E, work surface crochet over border round 1 of heart. Fasten off and sew in ends.

Using E and a tapestry needle, make 6 French knots (see page 123) in the centre of each flower (over round 1).

Sew all of the elements onto the heart, using the photograph as a guide. Fasten the polka dots in position using a French knot in E.

HANGING CORD

(make 2)
Using 3.5mm (US size E/4) hook and A, ch10, leaving a 15cm (6in) tail at either end.
Sew the tail ends of each length to the back of the heart near the top of each curve to make two concealed hanging loops to hook onto fixings on the wall.

Festive Baubles

Nestling one motif inside another doubles the colour opportunities, making this project a real feast for the senses. Notice how the white in round 3 creates a winter festive feel, whilst the all-colour ones are richer and deeper. Experiment with even more colour by replacing the gold and silver with contrasting colours instead and see where it takes you. The possibilities are endless!

Skill level: **

YARN AND MATERIALS

Rico Ricorumi DK (100% cotton, approx. 57m/62yd per 25g/⅞oz ball) DK (light worsted) weight yarn:

1 ball each of:
Candy Pink shade 012
Fuchsia shade 014
Orchid shade 016
Lilac shade 017
Pink shade 011
Light Blue shade 033
Turquoise shade 039
Blue shade 032
Grass Green shade 044
Emerald shade 042
Purple shade 020
Orange shade 027
Tangerine shade 026
Yellow shade 006
Light Green shade 046

Rico Ricorumi Lamé DK (62% polyester, 38% polyamide, approx. 50m/54yd per 10g/⅓oz ball) DK (light worsted) weight yarn:

1 ball each of:
Gold shade 002
Silver shade 001

HOOKS AND EQUIPMENT

3mm (US size C/2–D/3) crochet hook

Yarn needle

FINISHED MEASUREMENTS

5.5cm (2⅛in) wide x 3cm (1¼in) deep

TENSION

Round 1 measures 2cm (¾in) diameter using a 3mm (US size C/2–D/3) hook

ABBREVIATIONS

See page 127.

Inner layer

(make 12 in any colour combination)
Using first colour, make a magic ring.
Round 1: Ch3 (counts as first tr), 11tr in ring, ss in top of beg ch-3 to join. (*12 sts*)
Fasten off first colour.
Round 2: Join second colour in any st, ch2 (counts as first htr), 1htr in same st, 2htr in each st to end, ss in top of beg ch-2 to join. (*24 sts*)
Fasten off second colour.
Round 3: Join third colour in any st, ch2 (counts as first htr), 1htr in each st to end, ss in top of beg ch-2 to join.
Round 4: Using same colour, rep round 3.
Fasten off.

Outer layer

(make 12 in any colour combination)
Using first colour, make a magic ring.
Round 1: Ch3 (counts as first tr), 11tr in ring, ss in top of beg ch-3 to join. (*12 sts*)
Fasten off first colour.
Round 2: Join second colour in any st, ch3 (counts as first tr), 1tr in same st, 2tr in each st to end, ss in top of beg ch-3 to join. (*24 sts*)
Fasten off second colour.
Round 3: Join third colour in any st, ch2 (counts as first htr), 1htr in each st to end, ss in top of beg ch-2 to join.
Round 4: Using same colour, rep round 3.
Fasten off.

JOIN OUTER AND INNER LAYERS
Place inner layer inside the outer layer with WS tog.
Round 5: Using either Gold or Silver, and working into BLO of round 4 sts of inner layer and FLO of round 4 sts of outer layer, join yarn in any st, ch1

Tip

• Joining the two motifs can be fiddly to begin with but as you work round 5, gently sculpt them into shape and they will nest together beautifully.

COLOUR THERAPY

Notice how by framing each bauble in either silver or gold and matching this with the surface crochet in round 1, a degree of order is created.

(counts as first dc), 1dc in each of next 4 sts, 2dc in next st, [1dc in each of next 5 sts, 2dc in next st] 3 times, ss in beg ch-1 to join. (*28 sts*)
Fasten off.

Making up and finishing

Sew in any ends.

MAKE HANGING LOOP
Join same yarn as for round 5 in back of any dc, ch20, ss in same dc to join. Fasten off.

Balloon Bauble Bunting

I set out to create festive baubles, but once they were strung together I began to see them more as hot air balloons – hence their name! Whichever way you see them, the bright bursts of colour are held together by the gold border and mini beads.

Skill level: **

YARN AND MATERIALS

Rico Ricorumi DK (100% cotton, approx. 57m/62yd per 25g/⅞oz ball) DK (light worsted) weight yarn:
1 ball each of:
Candy Pink shade 012
Fuchsia shade 014
Orchid shade 016
Lilac shade 017
Pink shade 011
Berry shade 015
Purple shade 020
Wine Red shade 029
Orange shade 027
Tangerine shade 026
Blue shade 032
Sky Blue shade 031
Grass Green shade 044
Emerald shade 042
Yellow shade 006
Apricot shade 070
Nude shade 023
Light Green shade 046

Rico Ricorumi Lamé DK (62% polyester, 38% polyamide, approx. 50m/54yd per 10g/⅓oz ball) DK (light worsted) weight yarn:
1 ball of Gold shade 002

HOOKS AND EQUIPMENT

3mm (US size C/2–D/3) crochet hook
Yarn needle

FINISHED MEASUREMENTS

152cm (60in) long x 10cm (4in) deep

TENSION

Round 1 measures 2cm (¾in) diameter using a 3mm (US size C/2–D/3) hook.

ABBREVIATIONS

See page 127.

SPECIAL ABBREVIATIONS

4trCL (4-treble cluster): [yarn round hook, insert hook in stitch, yarn round hook, pull through the work, yarn round hook, pull through two loops on the hook] 4 times, yarn round hook and pull through all loops on hook to complete cluster
picot (make picot): ch4, ss in fourth ch from hook

Balloons

(make 14)
Using first colour, make a magic ring.
Round 1: Ch3 (counts as first tr), 11tr into ring, ss in top of beg ch-3 to join. (*12 sts*)
Fasten off first colour.
Round 2: Join second colour in any st, ch2 (counts as first htr), 1htr in same st, 2htr in each st around, ss in top of beg ch-2 to join. (*24 sts*)
Fasten off second colour.
Round 3: Join third colour in any st, ch2 (counts as htr), 2tr in next st, (1dtr, picot, ch1, 1dtr) in next st, 2tr in next st, [1htr in next st, 2htr in next st] 10 times, ss in top of beg ch-2 to join.
Fasten off third colour.
Round 4: Join gold in ch-1 sp before picot, ch1 (counts as dc), ch1, 1dc in ch-3 picot sp, ch3, 4trCL in third ch from hook, ch1, 1dc in next ch-1 sp (after picot), 1dc in each of next 6 sts, [2dc in next st, 1dc in each of next 2 sts] 4 times, (1dc, ch3, 1dc) in next st, [1dc in each of next 2 sts, 2dc in next st] 4 times, 1 dc in each of next 6 sts, ss in beg ch-1 to join.
Fasten off.

Mini beads

(make 15, in different colours)
Using any colour, make a magic ring, leaving 20cm (8in) tail end.

Round 1: Ch1 (does not count as a st), 6dc in magic ring. (*6 dc*)

Work in a continuous spiral.

Round 2: [2dc in next st] 6 times. (*12 dc*)

Round 3: 1dc in each of next 12 sts. (*12 dc*)

Round 4: [Dc2tog] 4 times, stuff bead with yarn tail, [dc2tog] twice. (*6 dc*)

Fasten off, weave tail in and out of rem sts, pull tight to close.

Making up and finishing

Sew in ends.

HANGING STRING

Using any colour, ch15, ss in fifteenth ch from hook to make hanging loop, ch15, 2dc in ch-3 sp of any balloon, *ch15, 2dc in ch-3 sp of next balloon; rep from * until all balloons are joined, ch30, ss in fifteenth ch from hook to make hanging loop.

Fasten off.

Using the corresponding colour for each mini bead in a yarn needle, join a mini bead at the mid-point of each ch-15 between the balloons.

Tip

• Apply spray starch and block each motif, or use a wash of PVA glue mixed with water to the back of the motifs to help them keep their shape.

Granny Bag

I had a lot of fun making this bag, primarily because the colours were a constant boost of positivity. It's fun to play with this project and follow your heart – and you may decide to choose an alternative key colour for round 5. I selected a beautiful amethyst colour, because I love how its depth and warmth frames the other colours. Notice the one simple colour rule throughout: round 3 is always a lighter version of round 4.

Skill level: *

YARN AND MATERIALS

Schoepjes Cahlista Aran Cotton (100% natural cotton, approx. 85m/93yd per 50g/1¾oz ball) aran (worsted) weight yarn:

  2 balls of Deep Amethyst shade
    508 (A)
  1 ball each of:
  Shocking Pink shade 114
  Tyrian Purple shade 128
  Royal Orange shade 189
  Yellow Gold shade 208
  Lemonade shade 403
  Lime Juice shade 392
  Crystalline shade 385
  Bluebell shade 173
  Cyan shade 397
  Jade shade 514
  Light Orchid shade 226
  Apple Granny shade 513

HOOKS AND EQUIPMENT

4mm (US size G/6) crochet hook

Yarn needle

4 stitch markers

FINISHED MEASUREMENTS

44cm (17¼in) wide x 36cm (14¼in) deep

51cm (20in) deep with handles

TENSION

Round 1 measures 3cm (1¼in) diameter using a 4mm (US size G/6) hook.

ABBREVIATIONS

See page 127.

Granny square

(make 24)
Using any colour, make a magic ring.

Round 1 (RS): Ch5 (counts as tr and ch2 throughout), [3tr, ch2] 3 times into ring, 2tr into ring, ss in third ch of beg ch-5 to join. (*Four 3-tr groups + 4 ch-2 sps*)
Fasten off first colour.

Round 2: Join second colour in any ch-2 sp, ch5, 3tr in same sp, [(3tr, ch2, 3tr) in next ch-2 sp] 3 times, 2tr in same sp as beg ch-5, ss in third ch of beg ch-5 to join. (*Eight 3-tr groups + 4 ch-2 sps*)
Fasten off second colour.

Round 3: Join third colour in any ch-2 sp, ch5, 3tr in same sp, *3tr in sp between 3-tr groups, (3tr, ch2, 3tr) in next ch-2 corner sp; rep from * twice more, 3tr in sp between 3-tr groups next ch-1 sp, 2tr in same sp as beg ch-5, ss in third ch of beg ch-5 to join. (*Twelve 3-tr groups + 4 ch-2 sps*)
Fasten off third colour.

Round 4: Join fourth colour in any ch-2 sp, ch4 (counts as 1htr and ch2), 2htr in same sp, *1htr in each of next 9 sts, (2htr, ch2, 2htr) in next ch-2 corner sp; rep from * twice more, *1htr in each of next 9 sts, (2htr, ch2, 1htr) in same sp as beg ch-4, ss in second ch of beg ch-4 to join. (*52 htr + 4 ch-2 sps*)
Fasten off fourth colour.

Round 5: Join A in any ch-2 sp, ch3 (counts as 1dc and ch2 throughout), 1dc in same sp, *1dc in each of next 13 sts, (1dc, ch2, 1dc) in next ch-2 corner sp; rep from * twice, 1dc in each of next 13 sts, 1dc in same sp as beg ch-3, ch2, ss in first ch of beg ch-3 to join. (*60 dc + 4 ch-2 sps*)
Fasten off A.

SEWING UP THE BAG

— — — — - fold line

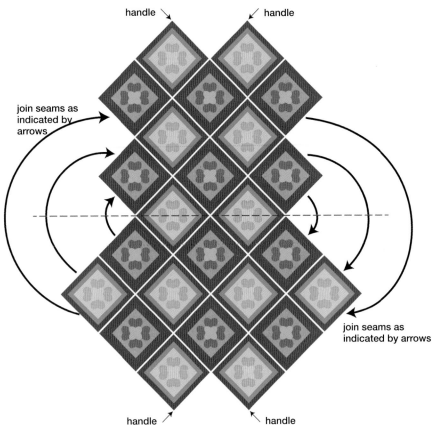

handle ↘   ↙ handle

join seams as
indicated by
arrows →

join seams as
indicated by arrows

handle ↗   ↖ handle

Making up and finishing

Lay all 24 squares in any sequence you choose following
the diagram for placement. Using A threaded in a yarn
needle, join the squares by holding two squares RS
together and sewing through the front loops only of round
5 stitches on both squares.

Once all the squares are joined, add a stitch marker in the
ch-2 corner sp of each of the two squares at either end
(these are where the handles will be). Fold the bag over
with RS together matching the seams as noted on the
diagram. Using A, sew the seams. Turn the bag RS out.

HANDLES
With RS facing, join A in marked ch-2 corner sp of first top
square on right of one side, ch3 (counts as 1dc and ch2),
1dc in same sp, *1dc in each of next 15 sts, move to next
square, 1dc in each of next 15 sts to next ch-2 corner sp,

(1dc, ch2, 1dc) in ch-2 corner sp; rep from * twice more,
1dc in each of next 15 sts, move to next square, 1dc in
each of next 15 sts to beg ch-2 corner sp, ss in first ch of
beg ch-3 to join.
Join in a second colour of your choice and hold together
with A as you cont:
Ch50 (or more if you want a longer handle), 1dc in ch-2
corner sp of next top square, ch1, turn, 1dc in same sp,
1dc in each ch working back to beg, 1dc in beg ch-2 sp.
Fasten off.
Rejoin yarn in ch-2 corner sp of top right square on
opposite side and repeat as for first handle.

Techniques

In this section, we explain how to master the simple crochet and finishing techniques that you need to make the projects in this book.

Holding the hook

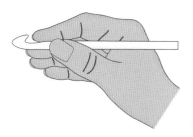

Pick up your hook as though you are picking up a pen or pencil. Keeping the hook held loosely between your fingers and thumb, turn your hand so that the palm is facing up and the hook is balanced in your hand and resting in the space between your index finger and your thumb.

You can also hold the hook like a knife – this may be easier if you are working with a large hook or with chunky yarn. Choose the method that you find most comfortable.

Holding the yarn

 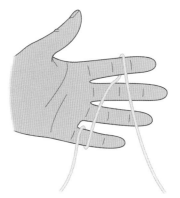

1 Pick up the yarn with your little finger in the opposite hand to your hook, with your palm facing upward and with the short end in front. Turn your hand to face downward, with the yarn on top of your index finger and under the other two fingers and wrapped right around the little finger, as shown above.

2 Turn your hand to face you, ready to hold the work in your middle finger and thumb. Keeping your index finger only at a slight curve, hold the work or the slip knot using the same hand, between your middle finger and your thumb and just below the crochet hook and loop/s on the hook.

Making a slip knot

The simplest way is to make a circle with the yarn, so that the loop is facing downward.

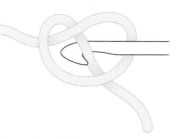 

1 In one hand hold the circle at the top where the yarn crosses, and let the end drop down at the back so that it falls across the centre of the loop. With your free hand or the tip of a crochet hook, pull a loop through the circle.

2 Put the hook into the loop and pull gently so that it forms a loose loop on the hook.

Yarn round hook (yrh)

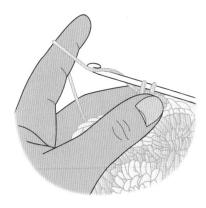

To create a stitch, catch the yarn from behind with the hook pointing upward. As you gently pull the yarn through the loop on the hook, turn the hook so it faces downward and slide the yarn through the loop. The loop on the hook should be kept loose enough for the hook to slide through easily.

Magic ring

This is a useful starting technique if you do not want a visible hole in the centre of your round. Loop the yarn around your finger, insert the hook through the ring, yarn round hook, pull through the ring to make the first chain. Work the number of stitches required into the ring and then pull the end to tighten the centre ring and close the hole.

Chain (ch)

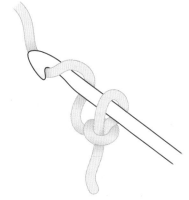

1 Using the hook, wrap the yarn round the hook ready to pull it through the loop on the hook.

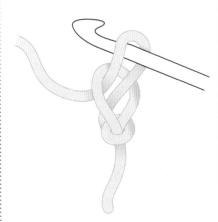

2 Pull through, creating a new loop on the hook. Continue in this way to create a chain of the required length.

Chain ring

If you are crocheting a round shape, one way of starting off is by crocheting a number of chains following the instructions in your pattern, and then joining them into a circle.

1 To join the chain into a circle, insert the crochet hook into the first chain that you made (not into the slip knot), yarn round hook.

2 Pull the yarn through the chain and through the loop on your hook at the same time, thereby creating a slip stitch and forming a circle. You now have a chain ring ready to work stitches into as instructed in the pattern.

Chain space (ch sp)

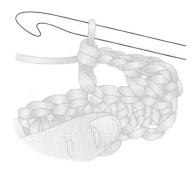

1 A chain space is the space that has been made under a chain in the previous round or row, and falls in between other stitches.

2 Stitches into a chain space are made directly into the hole created under the chain and not into the chain stitches themselves.

Slip stitch (ss)

A slip stitch doesn't create any height and is often used as the last stitch to create a smooth and even round or row.

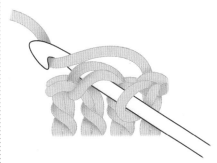

1 To make a slip stitch: first put the hook through the work, yarn round hook.

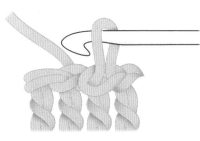

2 Pull the yarn through both the work and through the loop on the hook at the same time, so you will have 1 loop on the hook.

Making rounds

When working in rounds the work is not turned, so you are always working from one side. Depending on the pattern you are working, a 'round' can be square. Start each round by making one or more chains to create the height you need for the stitch you are working:
Double crochet = 1 chain
Half treble crochet = 2 chains
Treble crochet = 3 chains
Double treble = 4 chains
Work the required stitches to complete the round. At the end of the round, slip stitch into the top of the chain to close the round.

If you work in a spiral you do not need a turning chain. After completing the base ring, place a stitch marker in the first stitch and then continue to crochet around. When you have made a round and reached the point where the stitch marker is, work this stitch, take out the stitch marker from the previous round and put it back into the first stitch of the new round. A safety pin or piece of yarn in a contrasting colour makes a good stitch marker.

Making rows

When making straight rows you turn the work at the end of each row and make a turning chain to create the height you need for the stitch you are working with, as for making rounds.
Double crochet = 1 chain
Half treble crochet = 2 chains
Treble crochet = 3 chains
Double treble = 4 chains

Working into top of stitch

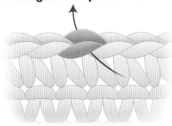

Unless otherwise directed, always insert the hook under both of the two loops on top of the stitch – this is the standard technique.

Working into front loop of stitch (FLO)

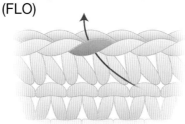

To work into the front loop of a stitch, pick up the front loop from underneath at the front of the work.

Working into back loop of stitch (BLO)

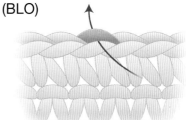

To work into the back loop of the stitch, insert the hook between the front and the back loop, picking up the back loop from the front of the work.

How to measure a tension (gauge) square

Using the hook and the yarn recommended in the pattern, make a number of chains to measure approximately 15cm (6in). Working in the stitch pattern given for the tension (gauge) measurements, work enough rows to form a square. Fasten off. Take a ruler, place it horizontally across the square and, using pins, mark a 10cm (4in) area. Repeat vertically to form a 10cm (4in) square on the fabric. Count the number of stitches across, and the number of rows within the square, and compare against the tension (gauge) given in the pattern.

If your numbers match the pattern then use this size hook and yarn for your project. If you have more stitches, then your tension (gauge) is tighter than recommended and you need to use a larger hook. If you have fewer stitches, then your tension (gauge) is looser and you will need a smaller hook.
Make tension (gauge) squares using different size hooks until you have matched that given in the pattern, and use this hook to make the project.

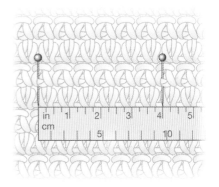

Double crochet (dc)

1 Insert the hook into your work, yarn round hook and pull the yarn through the work only. You will then have 2 loops on the hook.

2 Yarn round hook again and pull through the two loops on the hook. You will then have 1 loop on the hook.

Half treble crochet (htr)

1 Before inserting the hook into the work, wrap the yarn round the hook and put the hook through the work with the yarn wrapped around.

2 Yarn round hook again and pull through the first loop on the hook. You now have 3 loops on the hook.

3 Yarn round hook and pull the yarn through all 3 loops. You will be left with 1 loop on the hook.

Treble crochet (tr)

1 Before inserting the hook into the work, wrap the yarn round the hook. Put the hook through the work with the yarn wrapped around, yarn round hook again and pull through the first loop on the hook. You now have 3 loops on the hook.

2 Yarn round hook again, pull the yarn through the first 2 loops on the hook. You now have 2 loops on the hook.

Double treble (dtr)

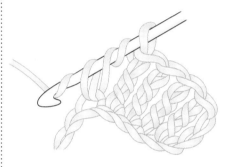

Yarn round hook twice, insert the hook into the stitch, yarn round hook, pull a loop through (4 loops on hook), yarn round hook, pull the yarn through 2 stitches (3 loops on hook), yarn round hook, pull a loop through the next 2 stitches (2 loops on hook), yarn round hook, pull a loop through the last 2 stitches. You will be left with 1 loop on the hook.

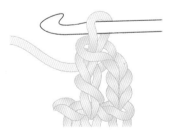

3 Pull the yarn through 2 loops again. You will be left with 1 loop on the hook.

Triple treble (trtr)

Triple trebles are 'tall' stitches and are an extension on the basic treble stitch. They need a turning chain of 5 chains.

1 Yarn round hook three times, insert the hook into the stitch or space. Yarn round hook, pull the yarn through the work (5 loops on hook).

2 Yarn round hook, pull the yarn through the first 2 loops on the hook (4 loops on hook).

3 Yarn round hook, pull the yarn through the first 2 loops on the hook (3 loops on hook).

4 Yarn round hook, pull the yarn through the first 2 loops on the hook (2 loops on hook). Yarn round hook, pull the yarn through the 2 loops on the hook. You will be left with 1 loop on the hook.

Extended double crochet (edc)

For these stitches you work a normal crochet stitch but into a stitch that is one, two or more rows below, which creates a V of yarn on the surface. They are sometimes called long stitches or spike stitch. These instructions are for an extended double crochet stitch (edc) but the same technique is used for other stitches such as extended treble or extended double treble.

 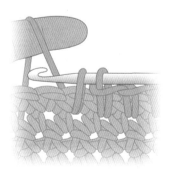 

1 Using a contrast yarn, insert your hook into the space one row below the next stitch – this is the top of the stitch one row below, so the same place that the stitch in the previous row is worked.

2 Yarn round hook and draw a loop up so it's level with the original loop on your hook.

3 Yarn round hook and pull through both loops to complete the extended double crochet.

Working around the posts

Stitches can be worked around the front post (FP) or back post (BP). These instructions show a treble being worked around the front post and back post, but you can work other stitches around the post in the same basic way.

FRONT POST TREBLE (FPtr)

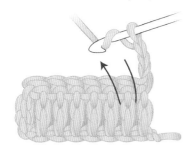 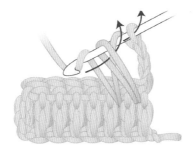 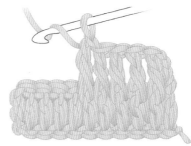

1 Yarn round hook and insert the hook from the front and around the post (the stem) of the next treble from right to left.

2 Yarn round hook and pull the yarn through the work, yarn round hook and pull the yarn through the first 2 loops on the hook.

3 Yarn round hook and pull the yarn through the 2 loops on the hook (1 loop on hook). One front post treble completed.

BACK POST TREBLE (BPtr)

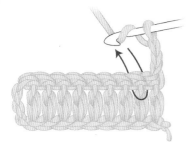 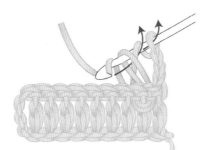 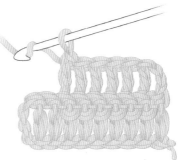

1 Yarn round hook and insert the hook from the back and around the post (the stem) of the next treble as directed in the pattern from right to left.

2 Yarn round hook and pull the yarn through the work, yarn round hook and pull the yarn through the first 2 loops on the hook.

3 Yarn round hook and pull the yarn through the 2 loops on the hook (1 loop on hook). One back post treble completed.

Popcorn stitch (PC)

This example shows a popcorn made with four treble stitches worked into a foundation chain, but a popcorn can be worked into any stitch or space and can be made up of any practical number or combination of stitches.

1 Inserting the hook in the same place each time, work four complete trebles.

2 Slip the hook out of the last loop and insert it into the top of the first stitch.

3 Then insert the hook into the loop of the last stitch again. Yarn round hook and pull it through as indicated.

4 This makes one complete popcorn.

Clusters (CL)

Clusters are groups of stitches, with each stitch only partly worked and then all joined at the end to form one stitch that creates a particular pattern and shape. Shown here is a three-treble cluster, but for four- or five-treble clusters, simply repeat steps 1 and 2 more times.

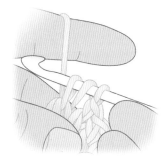

1 Yarn round hook, insert the hook in the stitch (or space). Yarn round hook, pull the yarn through the work (3 loops on hook).

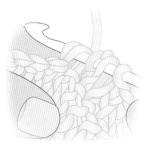

2 Yarn round hook, pull the yarn through 2 of the loops on the hook. Yarn round hook, insert the hook in the same stitch (or space).

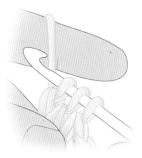

3 Yarn round hook, pull the yarn through the work (4 loops on hook). Yarn round hook, pull the yarn through 2 of the loops on the hook (3 loops on hook).

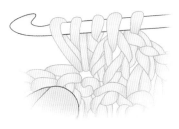

4 Yarn round hook, insert the hook in the same stitch (or space), yarn round hook, pull the yarn through the work (5 loops on hook).

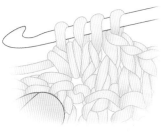

5 Yarn round hook, pull the yarn through 2 of the loops on the hook (4 loops on hook).

6 Yarn round hook, pull the yarn through all 4 loops on the hook (1 loop left on hook). One three-treble cluster made.

Puff stitch (PS)

A puff stitch is a padded stitch worked by creating several loops on the hook before completing the stitch. The basic principle is always the same, but you can repeat steps 1 and 2 fewer times to make a smaller puff. Sometimes a chain is worked at the end to secure the puff.

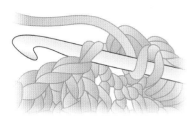

1 Yarn round hook, and insert the hook into the next stitch or space.

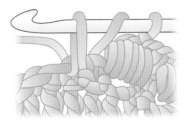

2 Yarn round hook again and draw through, keeping the loops of yarn long.

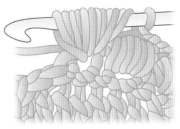

3 Repeat steps 1 and 2 five more times, keeping the loops long each time. There will be 13 loops on the hook.

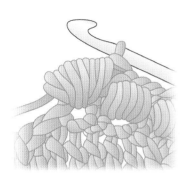

4 Yarn round hook and draw through all the loops on the hook.

5 Yarn round hook, and draw through the single loop on the hook to make a chain and secure the puff stitch.

Make bobble (MB)

A bobble is similar to a puff stitch, but you work a complete stitch at the start and then continue taking the yarn round the hook and drawing through the stitch to make the bobble as large as you like. Sometimes a chain is worked at the end to secure the bobble.

1 Yarn round the hook and insert the hook into the next stitch.

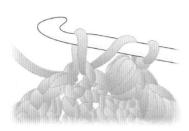

2 Yarn round hook and draw through the stitch.

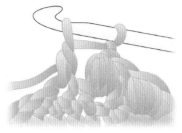

3 Yarn round hook, and draw through the first two loops on the hook.

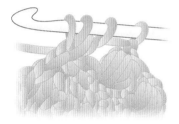

4 Yarn round the hook, insert the hook into the same stitch, yarn round hook and draw through the stitch.

5 Repeat step 4 three more times, keeping the loops long. There will be 10 loops on the hook. Wrap the yarn around the hook.

6 Then draw the yarn through all the loops on the hook to complete the bobble stitch.

Increasing

Make two or three stitches into one stitch or space from the previous row. The illustration shows a treble crochet increase being made.

Decreasing

You can decrease by either missing the next stitch and continuing to crochet, or by crocheting two or more stitches together. The basic technique for crocheting stitches together is the same, no matter which stitch you are using. The following example shows dc2tog.

DOUBLE CROCHET TWO STITCHES TOGETHER (dc2tog)

1 Insert the hook into your work, yarn round hook and pull the yarn through the work (2 loops on hook). Insert the hook in next stitch, yarn round hook and pull the yarn through.

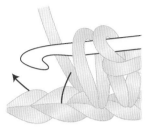

2 Yarn round hook again and pull through all 3 loops on the hook. You will then have 1 loop on the hook.

Joining yarn at the end of a row or round

You can use this technique when changing colour, or when joining in a new ball of yarn as one runs out.

1 Keep the loop of the old yarn on the hook. Drop the end and catch a loop of the strand of the new yarn with the crochet hook.

2 Draw the new yarn through the loop on the hook, keeping the old loop drawn tight and continue as instructed in the pattern.

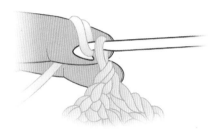

Joining in new yarn after fastening off

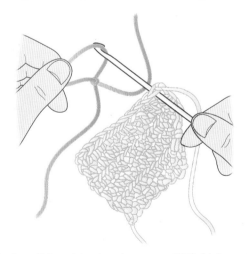

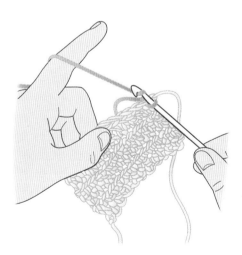

1 Fasten off the old colour (see page 123). Make a slip knot with the new colour (see page 111). Insert the hook into the stitch at the beginning of the next row, then through the slip knot.

2 Draw the loop of the slip knot through to the front of the work. Carry on working using the new colour, following the instructions in the pattern.

Joining yarn in the middle of a row or round

For a neat colour join in the middle of a row or round, use these methods.

JOINING A NEW COLOUR INTO DOUBLE CROCHET

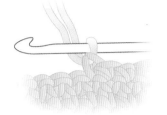 

1 Make a double crochet stitch (see page 114), but do not draw the final loop through, so there are 2 loops on the hook. Drop the old yarn, catch the new yarn with the hook and draw it through both loops to complete the stitch and join in the new colour at the same time.

2 Continue to crochet with the new yarn. Cut the old yarn leaving a 15cm (6in) end and weave the end in (see right) after working a row, or once the work is complete.

JOINING A NEW COLOUR INTO TREBLE CROCHET

1 Make a treble crochet stitch (see page 115), but do not draw the final loop through, so there are 2 loops on the hook. Drop the old yarn, catch the new yarn with the hook and draw it through both loops to complete the stitch and join in the new colour at the same time.

2 Continue to crochet with the new yarn. Cut the old yarn leaving a 15cm (6in) end and weave the end in (see right) after working a row, or once the work is complete.

Join-as-you-go method

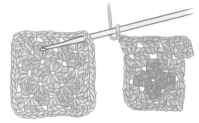 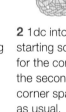 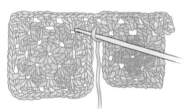 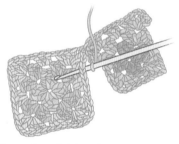

1 Work the first side of the current square including the first corner grouping (first set of 3htr or 3tr), then instead of making ch2 for the corner space, insert the hook into the corner space of the starting square from underneath as shown.

2 1dc into the corner space of the starting square (counts as first of 2-ch for the corner space), ch1, then work the second 3htr or 3tr grouping into the corner space of the current square as usual.

3 To continue joining the squares together, instead of ch1, work 1dc into the next side space of the starting square.

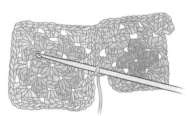 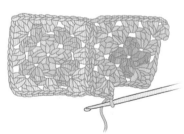 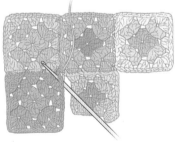

4 Work 3htr or 3tr in the next side space of the current square. Continue replacing each ch-1 at the sides of the current square with 1dc into the next side space of the starting square, and replacing the first of the ch-2 at the corner space of the current square with 1dc into the corner space of the starting square.

5 When the current square is joined to the starting square along one side, continue around and finish the final round of the current square as normal.

6 When joining a current square to two previous squares, replace both corner ch of the current square with 1dc into each adjoining square.

Enclosing a yarn end

You may find that the yarn end gets in the way as you work; you can enclose this into the stitches as you go by placing the end at the back as you wrap the yarn. This also saves having to sew this yarn end in later.

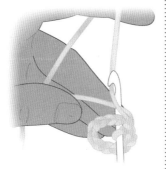

Fastening off

When you have finished crocheting, you need to fasten off the stitches to stop all your work unravelling.

1 Draw up the final loop of the last stitch to make it bigger. Cut the yarn, leaving an end of approximately 10cm (4in) – unless a longer end is needed for sewing up. Pull the end all the way through the loop and pull the loop up tightly.

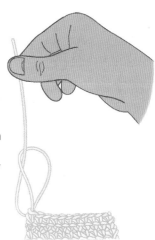

Weaving in yarn ends

It is important to weave in the ends of the yarn so that they are secure and your crochet won't unravel. Thread a yarn needle with the yarn end. On the wrong side, take the needle through the crochet one stitch down on the edge, then take it through the stitches, working in a gentle zig-zag. Work through four or five stitches then return in the opposite direction. Remove the needle, pull the crochet gently to stretch it and trim the end.

Making a French knot

Bring the needle up from the back of the fabric to the front. Wrap the thread two or three times around the tip of the needle, then reinsert the needle at the point where it first emerged, holding the wrapped threads with the thumbnail of your non-stitching hand, and pull the needle all the way through. The wraps will form a knot on the surface of the fabric.

Blocking

When making some of the projects, such as garlands or mandalas, you will find that taking the time to block and stiffen each crochet element will make a huge difference to the finished effect of your work. Without either of these processes you will find that the crochet will curl out of shape and lose its definition.

For a quick and easy way to block your crochet you'll need blocking pins, some soft foam mats (such as the ones sold as children's play mats) and some ironing spray starch. Pin each item out to shape and size onto the mats and then spray with the starch. Allow to dry for a day before attaching the elements to your garland or mandala.

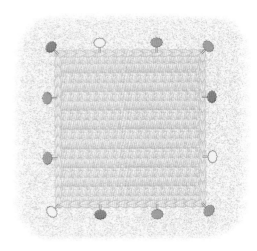

Making an oversewn seam

An oversewn join gives a nice flat seam and is the simplest and most common joining technique.

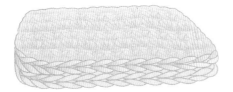

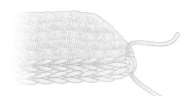

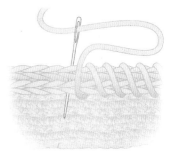

1 Thread a yarn sewing needle with the yarn you're using in the project. Place the pieces to be joined with right sides together.

2 Insert the needle in one corner in the top loops of the stitches of both pieces and pull up the yarn, leaving an end of about 5cm (2in). Go into the same place with the needle and pull up the yarn again; repeat two or three times to secure the yarn at the start of the seam.

3 Join the pieces together by taking the needle through the loops at the top of the corresponding stitches on each piece to the end. Fasten off the yarn at the end, as in step 2.

Making a double crochet seam

With a double crochet seam you join two pieces together using a crochet hook and working a double crochet stitch through both pieces, instead of sewing them together with a yarn end and a yarn sewing needle. This makes a quick and strong seam and gives a slightly raised finish to the edging. For a less raised seam, follow the same basic technique, but work each stitch in slip stitch rather than double crochet.

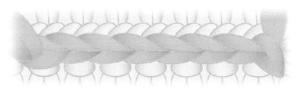

1 Start by lining up the two pieces with wrong sides together. Insert the hook in the top 2 loops of the stitch of the first piece, then into the corresponding stitch on the second piece.

2 Complete the double crochet stitch as normal and continue on the next stitches as directed in the pattern. This gives a raised effect if the double crochet stitches are made on the right side of the work.

3 You can work with the wrong side of the work facing (with the pieces right side facing) if you don't want this effect and it still creates a good strong join.

Sewing up with whip stitch

Whip stitch is an easy way to join pieces, but you will be able to see the stitches clearly, so use a matching yarn. Lay the two pieces to be joined next to each other with right sides facing upward. Secure the yarn to one piece. Insert the needle into the front of the fabric, then up from the back of the adjoining fabric. Repeat along the seam.

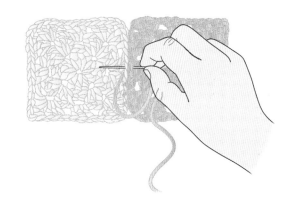

Making pompoms

1 Using a pair of card rings cut to the size of the pompom you would like to create, cut a length of yarn and wind it around the rings until the hole in the centre is filled.

2 Cut through the loops around the outer edge of the rings and ease them slightly apart. Thread a length of yarn between the layers of card and tie tightly, leaving a long end. Remove the card rings and fluff up the pompom. The long yarn end can be used to sew the pompom in place.

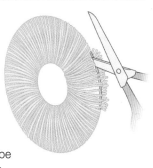

Making a tassel

1 Cut a piece of cardboard to the required length for the tassel, to wrap the yarn around. Cut four strands of yarn before you start, three approximately 6cm (2½in) long and another approximately 30cm (12in) long. Wrap the remaining yarn neatly around the cardboard about 25 times.

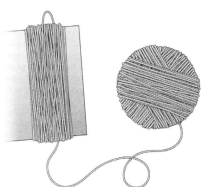

2 Take the three shorter lengths of yarn, and thread them through all the loops at the top.

3 Hold these pieces as you slide the loops off the cardboard, and then tie them tightly in a double knot.

4 Take the longer length of yarn cut earlier and tie it around the tassel, approx. 2.5cm (1in) from the top. Wrap around tightly several times and tie a tight knot. Trim the ends to match the ends of the tassel.

5 Cut the loops at the bottom of the tassel. Plait (braid) together the strands of yarn threaded through the top of the tassel, and tie a double knot at the end of the braid. Trim the ends to match the ends of the tassel.

Surface crochet

Surface crochet is a simple way to add extra decoration to a finished item, working slip stitches over the surface of the fabric.

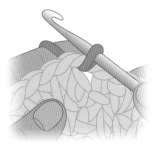 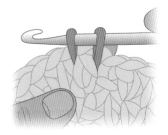 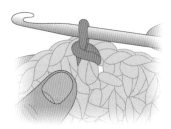

1 Using a contrast yarn, make a slip knot. Holding the yarn with the slip knot behind the work and the hook in front, insert the hook between two stitches from front to the back and catch the slip knot behind the work with the hook. Draw the slip knot back through, so there is 1 loop on the hook at the front of the work.

2 Insert the hook between the next 2 stitches, yarn round hook and draw a loop through to the front. You will now have 2 loops on the hook.

3 Pull the first loop on the hook through the second loop to complete the first slip stitch on the surface of the work.

Repeat steps 2 and 3 to make the next slip stitch. To join two ends with an invisible join, cut the yarn and thread onto a yarn needle. Insert the needle up through the last stitch, into the first stitch as if you were crocheting it, then into the back loop of the previous stitch. Fasten off on the wrong side.

Beading

When using beads, they must all be threaded onto the yarn before you start crocheting. Beads are placed when working with the wrong side of the work facing you. The beads will sit at the back of the work, and so appear on the front (right side).

1 When a bead is needed, slide it up the strand toward the back of the work so it's ready to place in the right part of the stitch you are working.

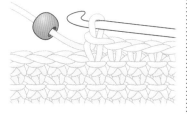

2 Work the stitch as indicated in the pattern. This will secure the bead at the back.

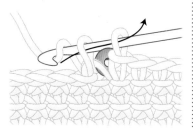

CROCHET STITCH CONVERSION CHART

Crochet stitches are worked in the same way in both the UK and the USA, but the stitch names are not the same and identical names are used for different stitches. Below is a list of the UK terms used in this book, and the equivalent US terms.

UK TERM	US TERM
double crochet (dc)	single crochet (sc)
half treble (htr)	half double crochet (hdc)
treble (tr)	double crochet (dc)
double treble (dtr)	treble (tr)
triple treble (trtr)	double treble (dtr)
quadruple treble (qtr)	triple treble (trtr)
tension	gauge
yarn round hook (yrh)	yarn over hook (yo)

Abbreviations

approx.	approximately
beg	begin(ning)
BLO	back loop only
BP	back post
ch	chain
ch sp	chain space
cm	centimetre(s)
cont	continu(e)ing
dc	double crochet
dc2tog	double crochet 2 stitches together
dec	decreas(e)ing
dtr	double treble
edc	extended double crochet
FLO	front loop only
foll	follow(s)ing
FP	front post
g	gram(mes)
htr	half treble
htr2tog	half treble 2 stitches together
in	inch(es)
inc	increas(e)ing
m	metre(s)
mm	millimetre(s)
oz	ounce(s)
patt	pattern
PM	place marker
prev	previous
rem	remaining
rep	repeat
RS	right side
sp	space
ss	slip stitch
st(s)	stitch(es)
tog	together
tr	treble
trtr	triple treble
yds	yards
WS	wrong side
yrh	yarn round hook
[ ]	work section between square brackets number of times stated
*	asterisk indicates beginning of repeated section of pattern

Suppliers

For reasons of space we cannot cover all stockists, so please explore the local yarn shops and online stores in your own country.

UK
Deramores
www.deramores.com

Laughing Hens
Tel: +44 (0) 1829 740903
www.laughinghens.com

LoveCrafts
www.lovecrafts.com

Wool
Store in Bath.
+44 (0)1225 469144
www.woolbath.co.uk

Wool Warehouse
www.woolwarehouse.co.uk

Hobbycraft
www.hobbycraft.co.uk

John Lewis
Yarns and craft supplies
www.johnlewis.com

USA
Knitting Fever Inc.
www.knittingfever.com

WEBS
www.yarn.com

Jo-Ann Fabric and Craft Stores
Yarns and craft supplies
www.joann.com

Michaels
Craft supplies
www.michaels.com

AUSTRALIA
Black Sheep Wool 'n' Wares
Retail store and online
Tel: +61 (0)2 6779 1196
www.blacksheepwool.com.au

Sun Spun
Retail store
www.sunspun.com.au

YARN COMPANIES
Adriafil
www.adriafil.com

Cascade
Stockist locator on website
www.cascadeyarns.com

DMC
Stockist locator on website
www.dmc.com

Rico Design
Stockist locator on website
www.rico-design.de

Rowan Yarns
Stockist locator on website
www.knitrowan.com

Scheepjes
Stockist locator on website
www.scheepjes.com

Stylecraft
Stockist locator on website
www.stylecraft-yarns.co.uk

West Yorkshire Spinners
Stockist locator on website
www.wyspinners.com

If you wish to substitute a different yarn for the one recommended in the pattern, try www.yarnsub.com for suggestions.

Acknowledgements

My thanks to Cindy Richards, Penny Craig, and the team at CICO Books for all your support, and to Marie Clayton and Jemima Bicknell for making the patterns coherent! Thanks also to James Gardiner and Nel Haynes for the beautiful photography and styling.

This book is an expression of my gratitude to the following people who continue to support and inspire: my friend and yarn mentor Michael Armstrong for your invaluable input and guidance; Amanda Bloom for making me a part of the Little Box of Crochet family; Sara Huntington for stretching my skills and feeding me ideas; Fran Morgan for keeping it real and making me laugh; and Rosie Wilks for your extraordinary skills with all things mathematical (our yarn bomb bus would never have made it without you). Thank you Marion Bedford for passing on your embroidery skills and giving me access to your stash of threads – the French knot is here to stay!

Sincere love and gratitude to Joe Macnab for teaching me to breathe, treating my repetitive-strain crochet injuries and leading me down the rabbit hole. Big love to my family for the endless love and encouragement and last but not least Rick and Lili, who share their life and space with this yarn-obsessed crazy cat lady… I salute you!

This colourful journey was made possible thanks to the generosity of Rico Design, Scheepjes and West Yorkshire Spinners, who continue to support me with bundles of yarn and colourful commissions… keep them coming!

Index

a
abbreviations 127

b
back post treble (BPtr) 117
bags and purses
    Granny Bag 108–110
    Striped Purses 58–59
    Woodland Walk Shoulder
        Bag 48–50
    Zipped Make-up Bags
        38–39
Balloon Bauble Bunting
    106–107
baubles
    Balloon Bauble Bunting
        106–107
    Festive Baubles 104–105
Beach-hut Bunting 13–15
beading 126
    Dreamcatcher 80–82
    Summer Spice Tassel Key
        Rings 36–37
blocking 123
Blue Tile Trivet 71–73
Bobble Cushion 74–75
Bobble Hat 76–77
bobbles (MB) 120
bunting
    Balloon Bauble Bunting
        106–107
    Beach-hut Bunting 13–15
    Festival Bunting 94–96

c
Carnival Shelf Valance 30–33
chain (ch) 112
chain ring 112
chain space (ch sp) 113
clusters (CL) 118
Coat Hangers 16–17
Colourplay Face Scrubbies
    34–35
cushions
    Bobble Cushion 74–75
    Floral Tiles Cushion 18–21
    Mandala Cushion 43–45
    Moroccan Floor Cushion
        91–93

d
decreasing 121
Dingle Dangle Garland 54–57
double crochet (dc) 114
    extended double crochet
        (edc) 116
    double crochet seam 124

double treble (dtr) 115
Dreamcatcher 80–82

e
extended double crochet
    (edc) 116

f
face scrubbies 34–35
fastening off 123
Festival Bunting 94–96
Festive Baubles 104–105
Floral Tiles Cushion 18–21
French knot 123
front post treble (FPtr) 117

g
garland 54–57
Gift Tags 22–23
gloves 51–53
Granny Bag 108–110

h
half treble crochet (htr) 115
hanging decorations
    Balloon Bauble Bunting
        106–107
    Beach-hut Bunting 13–15
    Dingle Dangle Garland
        54–57
    Dreamcatcher 80–82
    Festival Bunting 94–96
    Festive Baubles 104–105
    Namaste Heart 100–103
    Neon Mandalas 68–70
    Summer Love Wall Hanging
        40–42
hat 76–77
headband 64–65
holding
    hook 111
    yarn 111
hook, holding 111

i–j
increasing 120
joining pieces
    double crochet seam 124
    oversewn seam 124
    sewing up with whip stitch
        125

k
key rings 36–37

m
magic ring 112

mandalas
    Carnival Shelf Valance
        30–33
    Dreamcatcher 80–82
    Mandala Cushion 43–45
    Neon Mandalas 68–70
    Snowdrift Throw 83–85
    Summer Spice Tassel Key
        Rings 36–37
Moroccan Floor Cushion
    91–93

n–o
Namaste Heart 100–103
necklace 26–27
Neon Mandalas 68–70
oversewn seam 124

p
Patchwork Gloves 51–53
picture 88–90
pompoms 125
popcorn stitch (PC) 117
puff stitch (PS) 119

r
Rope Baskets 78–79
rounds
    joining yarn at end of row
        or round 121
    joining yarn in the middle or
        a row or round 122
    making 113
rows
    joining yarn at end of row
        or round 121
    joining yarn in the middle or
        a row or round 122
    making 113

s
scarves and cowls
    Season's End Scarf 60–61
    Speckled Cowl 62–63
seams
    double crochet seam 124
    oversewn seam 124
Season's End Scarf 60–61
shelf valance 30–33
slip knot 111
slip stitch (ss) 113
Snowdrift Throw 83–85
Speckled Cowl 62–63
Spring Blossom 24–25
Springtime Table Runner
    10–12
stitch conversion chart 126

stool 97–99
storage baskets 78–79
Striped Purses 58–59
Summer Love Wall Hanging
    40–42
Summer Spice Tassel Key
    Rings 36–37
suppliers 127
surface crochet 126

t
table runner 10–12
tassels 125
techniques 111–126
tension (gauge) square 114
    measuring 114
throw 83–85
treble crochet (tr) 115
    working around the posts
        117
triple treble (trtr) 116
trivet 71–73
Twisted Headband 64–65

v–w
Vase of Flowers 88–90
wall hanging 40–42
weaving in yarn ends 123
whip stitch 125
Winter Turns to Spring
    Necklace 26–27
Woodland Walk Shoulder
    Bag 48–50
working around the posts 117
working into back loop of
    stitch (BLO) 114
working into front loop of
    stitch (FLO) 114
working into top of stitch 114

y
yarn
    enclosing yarn end 123
    fastening off 123
    holding 111
    join-as-you-go method 122
    joining at end of row or
        round 121
    joining in middle or a row or
        round 122
    joining in new yarn 121
    weaving in yarn ends 123
Yarn-bombed Stool 97–99
yarn round hook (yrh) 112

z
Zipped Make-up Bags 38–39